PREFACE

By Dr. Kennedy, author of "Brain Reboot: A Change in Mind Will Change Your Brain."

In every corner of the world, irrespective of culture or upbringing, there is a relentless drive to improve, adapt, learn, and lead. This urge to progress is deeply embedded in the human psyche and is the basis for our greatest accomplishments as a species. Marlene Gonzalez's new book, "Brain Boost: A Neuro-Executive Coaching Model for Professional Development," embodies that quest for advancement — a modern-day guide to unlocking the leadership potential within each of us.

When I penned "Brain Reboot," I delved into the astonishing plasticity of the human brain, illustrating how minor shifts in mindset could literally rewire our neural pathways. My central premise was that to change one's mind is to change the brain itself. In her transformative work, Gonzalez seamlessly takes this foundational knowledge to the next frontier: Brain-based leadership.

In the past, the qualities that defined a leader were often seen as mysterious and elusive. But what if leadership wasn't just about charisma, innate talent, or fate? What if the crux of great leadership lies in the very organ that defines our humanity— our brain? And what if the key to becoming an effective leader wasn't about being born with a particular gene but about understanding and harnessing the power of our own neuroplasticity?

"Brain Boost" is not just a testament to the incredible potential of brain-based coaching; it's also a celebration of the resilience and vigor of Latino leaders in Corporate America and beyond. Marlene's rich tapestry of testimonials and actionable insights sheds light on the often underrepresented and untapped potential of Latino, female, and other minority professionals in leadership roles.

Throughout this book, you will encounter narratives that resonate with the human experience's universality while providing a tailored roadmap for Latino leaders. It is a journey that weaves neuroscience, personal anecdotes, and actionable strategies into a cohesive whole. A journey that validates that irrespective of one's cultural background or the adversities faced, the brain remains our greatest ally. Anyone can tap into its limitless potential with the right tools, techniques, and knowledge.

As you venture into the depths of "Brain Boost," keep an open mind and heart. Allow Marlene's words to guide, inspire and challenge you. Let her insights catalyze your own brain reboot, reshaping your approach to leadership and life.

The human brain, with its billion-fold complexities, is our greatest asset. Let's harness its power, redefine leadership paradigms, and usher in an era of inclusive, empathetic, and effective leaders. The journey starts now. Embrace it.

PRAISE FOR MARLENE GONZALEZ

Domestic Editorial Reviews

"The leader of today is one that can handle the multitude of stressors including the influx of data quickly coming their way, and inevitable constant change. The only way we can be true leaders for ourselves, and others, is by mastering our own behaviors by tapping into the power in our heads – the brain! Marlene is the best person to release this book as she is a leadership development guru, leveraging the science of neuroplasticity to help us unleash our fullest leadership potential!."

Patricia Mota, President & CEO. Hispanic Alliance for Career Enhancement, HACE. USA

"Prepare to embark on a transformative journey with 'Brain Boost'. This book is a beacon of guidance for those eager to unlock their full potential for those aspiring to be a forward-thinker leader. Dive into 'Brain Boost' to explore your own potential and shape the future of your leadership."

Raquel Egusquiza, Executive Director. Latin Grammy Foundation. Miami, FL. USA.

"In 'Brain Boost,' Marlene González brilliantly bridges the gap between science and leadership. A tour de force of insight and actionable strategies, this book is a beacon for individuals seeking to elevate their cognitive prowess and leadership acumen. González not only offers readers a blueprint to a sharper mind but a path to unprecedented professional growth. A must-read for the forward-thinking leader."

Maribel Bulleri Product Lead. Merck & Co. USA

International Editorial Reviews

"In Marlene Gonzalez's narrative, we encounter a tale of triumph over adversity, as she journeys from overcoming childhood traumas to becoming an influential leader. Her challenging upbringing, marked by abandonment and adversities, didn't confine her; it shaped her into a leading CEO. More than her ascent, Marlene's unique melding of behavioral insights and neuroscience stands out. This book doesn't just share her story; it uncovers how neuroscience can amplify your leadership potential, demonstrating that success isn't predetermined by our past. With Marlene's insights, realize that leadership transformation isn't just a goal—it's a journey, and it starts with this very read. Dive in, and let Marlene be your beacon to leadership excellence." **Barry Downing, Executive Coach, Board Certified Master Neuroplastician, Neuro Coach, Neurofeedback Specialist/Mentor. Canada**

"In "Brain Boost," Marlene Gonzalez delves deep into how the brain's neuroplasticity influences leadership, pushing past conventional ideas of talents and traits. She emphasizes a growth mindset as key to personal and professional advancement. Embracing challenges, learning from errors, and valuing feedback can enhance our brain's functionality. Marlene shows how leaders with this mindset can transform teams, taking companies from stagnation to growth. They view setbacks as growth opportunities, fostering resilience. More than just theory, she offers practical steps to cultivate this mindset. "Brain Boost" is a must-read for visionary leaders."

Dr. Ignatius Odongo, Birmingham City University, United Kingdom.

"In the dynamic world of leadership development, "Brain Boost: Developing Leaders through Neuroplasticity" is a groundbreaking blend of neuroscience and executive coaching. This book, akin to a personal coach, introduces a neuro-executive coaching model to enhance leadership skills using scientific principles. Starting with a concise overview of brain anatomy, the text simplifies intricate concepts, setting the foundation for understanding neuroplasticity. The emphasis on fixed versus growth mindsets in leadership is enlightening. With real-world examples, the authors illustrate how mindset affects leadership and offer practical strategies for cultivating a growth mindset. The book's forte is its balance of theory and actionable insights, bridging scientific knowledge with its practical application in leadership. A must-read, it not only educates but empowers leaders to harness their brain's potential for effective leadership. Highly recommended for a comprehensive leadership development journey."

Kerstin Jatho, Coach and Facilitator 4 Seeds in South Africa.

INTRODUCTION

Imagine a world where exceptional leadership was all about luck, a genetic predisposition bestowed upon a special few. In that world, your genetic makeup would determine how well you execute your strategies, influence your decision-making and inform your risk-taking. If you wanted to go against the grain to try and achieve something truly great, you'd have to consult your doctor to know if you have the "it" gene. No matter what you did, without the right genetic makeup, all efforts to lead would be as pointless as boiling the ocean.

Fortunately, that world is imaginary and far from the truth. Only 10% of people are born with innate leadership abilities; even then, they must work hard to develop them. An additional 20% are born with fundamental managerial skills that can be nurtured and refined to attain top-tier leadership capabilities. The vast majority of leaders have attained their proficiency through rigorous training, hands-on experience and the guidance of seasoned mentors. They've worked incredibly hard to be great at leadership, and this is good news because it means that aspiring leaders willing to put in the work can embark on a transformative journey into excellent leadership.

Welcome to "Brain Boost: The Neuro-Executive Coaching Model for Professional Development." This book goes in-depth to explore brain-based coaching and uncover its immense potential for Latino leaders in Corporate America and the rest of the world. It's a book born from an intimate understanding of the challenges we have to grapple with as professionals trying to ascend executive levels, and that knowledge shapes the kinds of insights, strategies and tools you'll find here. The goal? To help you to navigate your journey into the C-suite successfully.

Think of this book as your coach. Whether you came here looking for tools to advance your career or to quench your thirst for knowledge, whether you're here hoping for guidance out of a rut or looking for inspiration to achieve a work-life balance, there is something for you within these pages. You'll find your decision to explore brain-based coaching to be pivotal. It will start you on a journey to true leadership, acknowledging that such leadership transcends cultural background or technical skills. It reaches deeper into the intricate world of emotions, brains and behaviors.

You'll be introduced to a neuro-executive coaching model, a groundbreaking approach that harnesses neuroscience's power to optimize brain function to achieve professional and personal goals. Traditionally, when you work with a coach, you get into a collaborative relationship. The coach acts as a creative partner, accountability partner, thinking partner and perhaps most importantly, a listening partner. Occasionally, when the situation calls for it, and depending on the type of coaching, the coach also plays the devil's advocate or takes on the role of a supporter or motivator. You will find these elements in this book, but they go beyond traditional coaching. The neuro-executive model discussed here combines the knowledge of psychology, brain anatomy and physiology to empower you to enhance your emotional intelligence and cognitive abilities while creating new habits for success.

Why should you care about this coaching model? As a leader, your influence demands you go beyond surface-level competencies and embody leadership. It demands a comprehensive blend of behavioral, emotional and cognitive skills. By leveraging the principles of neuropsychology, this book can get you there. You'll better understand your strengths and weaknesses, develop targeted strategies for improving performance and unlock your full leadership potential. When you optimize your brain function, you make better choices, communicate effectively and build stronger relationships with your teams, and what leader does not want that?

"Brain Boost" will set you on a transformative journey toward unlocking your true leadership potential. It's not just a collection of theoretical and scientific concepts but rather a practical guide of tried and tested shortcuts on your path to success. Each chapter has actionable strategies and insights from real-world experiences and extensive research. You'll find knowledge born from many years of study, exploration and application. The shortcuts in this book are a distillation of the latest advancements in organizational neuroscience and practical wisdom gained from guiding numerous Latino leaders through their professional development journeys.

As you go through these pages, you'll encounter many examples of people with first-hand experience using the different techniques forming parts of the neuro-executive coaching model. These stories illustrate the profound possibilities of this model if only you dare embrace its principles. Just think of a life where you aren't constrained by self-doubt or limited by your beliefs.

Envision a future where you lead teams, make impactful decisions and achieve remarkable success. That is the future this book will guide you toward — a life where you thrive as a Latino leader in Corporate America.

ABOUT THE AUTHOR

Marlene Gonzalez brings a wealth of experience and expertise to guide you on this journey. As a highly qualified executive coach and facilitator, she's dedicated herself to studying and developing transformational leadership. Marlene's first-hand experience as a first-generation Venezuelan American, coupled with her extensive executive positions in the United States, Europe and Latin America, gives her a unique perspective on Latino leaders' challenges and opportunities. Marlene holds a Bachelor of Science degree, an Executive PAG/EMBA and a graduate diploma for managerial issues in the global enterprise from Thunderbird University. Currently pursuing a Doctor of Business Administration in Organizational Neuroscience, Marlene is at the forefront of integrating cutting-edge research with practical applications to drive personal and professional growth.

In the following chapters, you'll uncover the difficulties leaders faced before the advent of brain-based coaching and how the insights shared here can bridge that gap. By the end of the book, you'll be grateful that you found the right coach for your journey. You will have the necessary skills and tools to step into your leadership future.

Now, let's get to it. Get ready to embark on this transformative exploration of brain-based coaching and unleash your true leadership potential. Get ready to boost your brainpower and revolutionize your professional development. Your journey starts here.

1

MASTERING THE BRAIN

Did you know that while the human brain constitutes only 2% of the body's weight, it accounts for 20% of its energy consumption? This fascinating fact sheds light on the relationship between mental activity and energy expenditure. Have you ever thought about what happens in your brain in terms of energy on days you spend time on the couch watching Netflix or skimming through social media? What about days when you're working hard, using your brain to solve problems and engage in other difficult mental activities? Do you burn more energy on your couch over a weekend or on a Wednesday afternoon spent problem-solving at work?

The short answer is that you spend more energy doing intense cognitive tasks at work than you do when surfing social media. Unlike other parts of your body, your brain runs exclusively on glucose. Strenuous cognitive activity requires more glucose than simple activity. For example, when you try to memorize something, the parts of your brain that deal with memory formation use more energy than the rest of the brain. In comparison, the difference in calories that you burn moving between mental tasks is tiny.

To put the calorie expenditure in perspective, unless you are a professional athlete, most of your body's energy expenditure doesn't have to do with exercise or movement. Between 8% and 15% of your energy goes to digestion, while a majority of the rest is used to power your organs, including the brain. No part of your body demands more energy than the brain. This means that you use about 320 calories on a regular day just to think.

Of course, different tasks and mental states affect the way your brain consumes energy. Research has shown that if your brain was scanned while you watched TV or worked on a word puzzle, brain activity would show that the more demanding mental task takes up more energy. This does not suggest that you could lose weight from doing challenging mental work. Against the backdrop of all brain activity, the change in energy expenditure would compound to about 5% on a good day. Even if you were to spend the whole day doing tough cognitive work, the 5% would not add up to much, calorie-wise. It is the equivalent of the energy you expend pacing in your office.

It's also worth noting that the bulk of the brain's energy consumption goes toward keeping you alert, watching your environment to take in important information and managing other internal activities. That is to say that the thought you have is cheap, but the system/machinery that makes the idea is super expensive. After a sustained period of intense cognitive work, your brain's ability to focus dwindles as your body's glucose levels decrease.

This chapter will help you understand how your brain works from an anatomical perspective. It discusses the physiology of the brain, the key structures involved in its function and how understanding the brain can help you improve your performance as a leader.

THE ANATOMY AND PHYSIOLOGY OF THE BRAIN

Weighing about 3 pounds, the brain controls all body functions, interprets outside information and embodies the essence of the soul and mind. Memory, emotion, intelligence and creativity are some of the functions governed by the brain. It controls speech, thoughts and movement as well as the function of many body organs. Generally speaking, the brain comprises three parts — the brainstem, cerebellum and cerebrum. It gets information from your five senses — touch, smell, sight, hearing and taste — and sometimes a lot of information at once. The brain takes that information and arranges it in a way that makes sense to you. Some of it gets stored in your memory.

Of the brain's total weight, close to 60% is fat. The rest is a combination of carbohydrates, water, salts and protein. Technically speaking, the brain is not a muscle. It has nerves and blood vessels, including glial cells and neurons. When you feel tired, for example, the brain picks up electrical and chemical signals and interprets them as fatigue. It also translates messages for pain, pleasure and so forth. There are messages the brain keeps and others that get relayed via the spine across the body's network of nerves.

Besides information from the five senses, your brain also receives input, such as temperature, vibration and pain from the rest of the body, together with autonomic or involuntary inputs from your organs. It interprets this information to help you understand and associate meaning to your thoughts, actions and feelings. Essentially, the brain enables memory, decisions, sensory perceptions, speech and language, movement, coordination and balance, stress responses and autonomic behavior like heart rate, breathing and organ function. Now, let's consider the different parts of the brain:

- **Cerebrum**

The cerebrum, located in the front of the brain, is made up of cerebral cortex (gray matter) and white matter at the center of the gray matter. It's the largest brain part and is responsible for regulating temperature and initiating and coordinating movement. Other features of the cerebrum enable problem-solving, judgment, speech, reasoning, learning and emotions while others relate to touch, hearing, vision and other senses. Gray matter has a larger surface area because of its folds, making up about 50% of the brain's weight.

The cerebrum is divided into two hemispheres, or halves, covered with folds and ridges. The hemispheres are joined by a fissure that runs from the front to the back of your head. The right hemisphere manages the left side of your body; the left hemisphere controls the right side. The two hemispheres communicate through the corpus callosum, a structure of nerve pathways and white matter.

For most people, the left-side hemisphere is the "dominant" hemisphere — as long as they are right-handed. If you are left-handed, the right side is dominant. Generally, the dominant hemisphere regulates your speech and language functions while the non-dominant side deals with special awareness, helping you process information taken in through your senses. There are exceptions, though. Nearly one in 10 right-handed people, and one in every three left-handed people, have a dominant right hemisphere, meaning that their speech functions are managed there. Often, this is a standard variant, but some people with epilepsy or brain tumors have had their dominance shift because of brain plasticity.

- **Brainstem**

The brainstem, or the middle of the brain, connects the cerebrum and spinal cord. It includes the medulla, pons and midbrain. The midbrain is a complex structure of neuron clusters and pathways that facilitate different functions, from movement and hearing to calculating response to environmental changes. The midbrain also has the nigra, an area that can be affected by Parkinson's disease because it is heavy in dopamine neurons and enables coordination and movement.

The pons is where the brain's 12 cranial nerves originate. It enables different activities such as chewing, tear production, vision focus, facial expressions, balance and hearing. The pons connects the medulla and the midbrain.

The medulla is located at the end of the brainstem, creating the meeting point for your spinal cord and brain. It is necessary for survival, regulating body activities like oxygen and carbon (IV) oxide levels, heart rhythm, breathing and blood flow. The medulla produces reflex activities like swallowing, sneezing, coughing and vomiting. The spinal cord stretches from the medulla through an opening in the skull and along your body, carrying messages to and from the brain.

- **Cerebellum**

The cerebellum, or "little brain" as it is sometimes called, is about the size of a fist. It's located at the back of your head below the occipital and temporal lobes and above the brainstem. Like the cerebrum, the cerebellum has two hemispheres. Its outer side is made up of neurons and the inner side communicates with the cerebral cortex. The cerebellum coordinates voluntary muscle movements and maintains balance, posture and equilibrium.

Each of the two hemispheres in the cerebellum is divided into four sections known as lobes — occipital, temporal, parietal and frontal — and they all play specific roles. The frontal lobe is the largest and is located at the front. It is involved in movement, decision-making and personality formation and is part of the system that recognizes smell. The frontal lobe contains the Broca's areas (discussed in Chapter 8) associated with speech.

The parietal lobe, located in the middle, helps in object identification. It enables you to understand spatial relationships and interpret touch and body pain. It houses the Wernicke's area (discussed in Chapter 8) that helps you understand language. The occipital lobe is involved with vision while the temporal lobe is associated with speech, short-term memory and musical rhythm.

Parts of the Human Brain

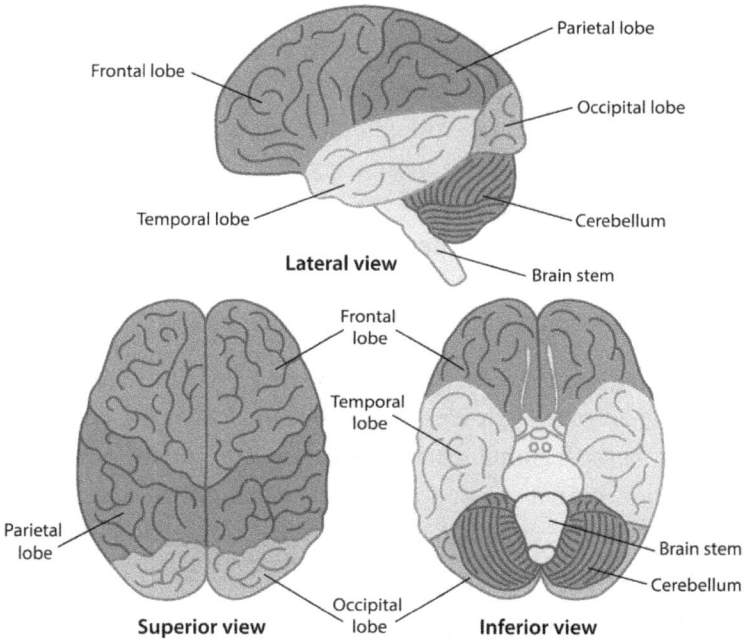

Parietal lobe

Frontal lobe

Occipital lobe

Temporal lobe

Cerebellum

Lateral view

Brain stem

Frontal lobe

Temporal lobe

Parietal lobe

Occipital lobe

Brain stem

Cerebellum

Superior view

Inferior view

Figure 1 Parts Of The Brain

THE LIMBIC SYSTEM

Your brain is very complex. It controls and coordinates every-thing you do, from your heart rate to your movements. It also plays a significant role in how you process and control your emotions. There is still much yet to be learned about emotions, but neuroscience has made great strides in how the brain — particularly the limbic system — controls emotions.

The limbic system is made up of different parts which play roles that impact your daily life. It includes the amygdala, hippocampus and hypothalamus.

For starters, the hippocampus comprises two parts, one in the left hemisphere and the other in the right. It draws its name from the Greek word describing its shape like a curvy seahorse. Essentially, the hippocampus controls your memory. It is where memories are made and stored. It has also been connected to emotions and learning. You can find the hippocampus in the temporal lobes just above your ear, which is arguably responsible for the hippocampus being the most researched part of the brain. It helps generate new neurons and is one of the few places where neurogenesis (the process through which new neurons are formed in the brain) happens.

Historically, the hippocampus was believed to be closely tied to the sense of smell. However, the notion has been debunked. Even so, because some smells trigger specific memories — like the smell of cinnamon and pumpkins getting linked to autumn — there is some evidence that there are connections between the hippocampus and the sense of smell.

Besides its role in forming memories, the hippocampus is responsible for navigating space and transferring long-term memories. When it's damaged in an accident, for example, people experience short-term memory loss, disorientation or forgetting things like words, locations and directions. Diseases like dementia and Alzheimer's have been linked with damage to the hippocampus.

Another part of the limbic system is the amygdala, an almond-shaped area next to the hippocampus. It helps the brain form new memories and works with the hippocampus to attach emotions to memories. However, its primary job is regulating and controlling emotional responses, handling feelings like happiness, anger and fear.

Because it connects emotions and memories, the amygdala helps you form strong and lasting memories. It has been found that memories driven by emotion tend to last over the long term compared to those with little emotional content. The amygdala is also responsible for emotional learning and has been linked to mental health disorders like addiction and anxiety. When the amygdala is damaged, people can struggle to form emotional memories. They may develop intense anxiety, irritability or aggression and experience intense responses to fear.

The hypothalamus has a primary function of homeostasis, helping to maintain and steady your body's internal state. It has been found to control autonomic functions, including body temperature, thirst, blood pressure and hunger. It also regulates sexual behavior, motivation and stress responses. To do its job, the hypothalamus works with different stimuli like odor, arousal, light and stress. When damaged, a person can become fatigued, stressed or aggressive. They experience changes in weight and sex drive as well as hypothermia and hyperthermia.

Hypothermia and hyperthermia are opposites. Hypothermia occurs when the body temperature falls below the required degree to maintain metabolism. Hyperthermia happens when the body absorbs or generates more heat than it can release (more than 38.7 degrees Celsius).

Limbic System

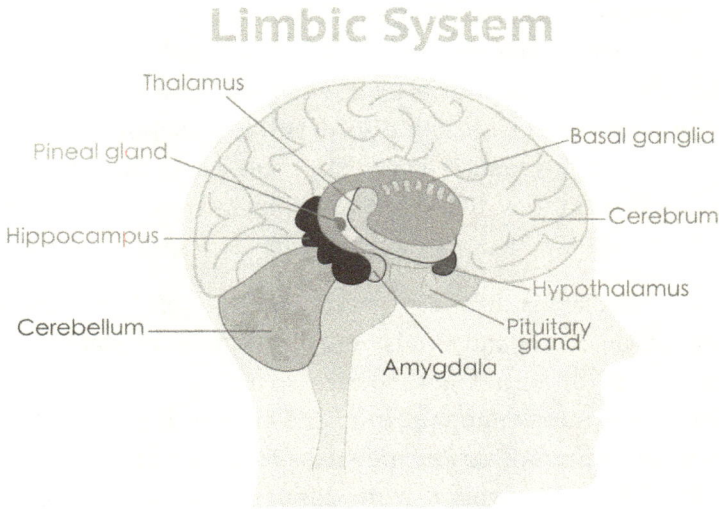

Thalamus

Pineal gland

Basal ganglia

Hippocampus

Cerebrum

Cerebellum

Hypothalamus

Pituitary gland

Amygdala

Figure 2 Limbic System

More about the limbic system

The limbic system, located inside the cerebrum — the largest part of the brain — has many roles and its different functions work together in one way or another. It is connected to your autonomic and endocrine nervous systems, playing a significant role in how your body responds to stressful environments and situations. The limbic system has been linked to survival instincts, including reproduction, hunger and eating, care for children and the fight-or-flight response.

To help you understand how the system's different parts work together, consider fear. Biologically speaking, this important emotion enables you to respond appropriately to threats. Fear is generated when the amygdala is stimulated, which then activates the hypothalamus to produce the fight-or-flight response. The hypothalamus signals your adrenal glands to release hormones like cortisol and adrenaline. Once these hormones enter the bloodstream, you notice physical changes like increased perspiration, faster breathing and raised heart rate. When you respond to a threat, the amygdala learns from it. It makes an association between the event and fear, allowing you to be prepared in the future.

The process is similar to anger. Anger is a response to stressors or threats within your environment. When you're in a dangerous situation that you can't escape, you likely respond with aggression or anger. It's no wonder the anger response is sometimes classified as part of the fight-or-flight response. Anger begins with the amygdala sending a signal to the hypothalamus. Parts of the prefrontal cortex then get involved. If their involvement is sufficient, you can regulate your anger response. When the prefrontal cortex is damaged, people may struggle to control their aggression or anger.

Clearly, the brain is very complex as an organ. Researchers and neuroscientists are still working to understand its operations, but what is known has vast implications for leadership development.

THE BRAIN IS THE FOUNDATION OF LEADERSHIP

For many years, leaders have worked to become more competent without fully understanding the brain's role in influencing behavior. They have been introduced to concepts like emotional intelligence and personality types as ways to develop behavioral competence. Still, these methods have not always been connected to how the brain functions, missing a significant part of the leadership equation. Often, leadership development programs have leaned toward personality assessments like the Myers-Briggs Type Indicator (MBTI) as tools for behavior change. People are left with valuable information but without learning what to do with it. The programs don't connect personality with the brain's neurophysiology. As a result, aspiring leaders fail to understand the area of their brain they're leading from and how it affects their behavior.

Often, personality assessments are meant to help you understand your behavior or that of an employee, and that's a good thing. Assessments fall short when they lack a clear approach to practice or understand the meaning of what's been provided. It doesn't help that results often fail to focus on the needs and functions associated with different behaviors. They end up producing statements of fact that lack empathy and don't engage you or the employee to understand and change the underlying conduct. This is why leaders should care about neuroscience. The brain controls all behavioral and cognitive functions necessary for leadership.

Brain scientists have found the brain has other parts that play different functions and influence your personality. People are meant to take advantage of all those parts to develop neural communication, but most personality-based leadership programs use only one aspect, falling short of the brain's potential. Imagine the positive impact on your leadership if you accessed and leveraged all parts of your brain.

Most of those in leadership roles tend to use the left hemisphere of the rational brain. This makes sense because that part is concerned with logical and rational decision-making. It analyzes, plans and organizes. However, many leaders fail to use the side of the brain meant for relating. As a result, they struggle to show appreciation, resolve conflict, manage performance and empathize — all activities that require the right side of the brain. This is one hurdle you can overcome by understanding the science of the brain.

Leaders can use their knowledge of the brain's workings to gain insight into emotional and cognitive processes. When a leader is aware of how their brain is organized, they can recognize their preferred behaviors and the gaps created when they do not develop their less automatized functions. Understanding neuroscience helps you become familiar with the needs and behaviors of your personality and those of others. It gives you insight into why people act as they do. This appreciation of differences helps you provide an environment where team members' personalities grow, ultimately creating a better and more productive work environment.

Understanding the brain can help you manage your biases and emotional responses as a leader. This, in turn, impacts your communication and decision-making. In difficult times or when you deal with uncertainty, your brain processes it as if you lack something that would allow you to adjust to the situation. If you aren't aware of how your brain works, you avoid uncertainty at all costs, even if it means you miss out on something potentially positive. Understanding neuroscience helps you better understand and manage risk.

Leaders who understand brain function can design more effective training and development programs because they know how people learn. Not only that but understanding the brain can help you have accountability conversations that involve receiving and giving feedback. The brain starts to see these interactions as social, signaling them as safe. As a result, you are engaged, sincere, genuine and honest. Neuroscience helps us to understand human behavior whether at work or home.

When you know how the brain functions, you are more adept at managing stress and building resilience, which are necessary for effective leadership. You can better create a culture that helps everyone — a culture of creativity and innovation. Brains are complex, but neuroscience shows that small actions make a huge difference. As a leader aware of this, you never have to wait for significant cultural shifts in your organization. You can begin applying the knowledge immediately and in small ways to create a better environment for everyone.

Finally, leaders who understand neuroscience can leverage brain-based strategies and insights to improve their emotional and cognitive skills, leading to better communication, improved decision-making and enhanced overall performance. The brain is incredibly agile — it can change, restructure and learn — and a knowledge of neuroscience allows you to leverage those features. It enables you to keep learning well into old age.

Clearly, there's a lot to learn about the brain, whether it has to do with its different parts and functions or how each area influences behavior. It is also clear that the brain is the foundation for leadership. Any attempts to change behavior or improve leadership without this in mind are near-sighted and unsustainable. You have to begin with neuroscience. One of the brain's biggest strengths is its neuroplasticity or ability to keep restructuring and learning. Let us explore that in the next chapter.

2

THE POWER OF THE MIND

Have you ever wondered how successful people achieve their remarkable accomplishments? Do you believe their success stems solely from innate gifts, talents or intelligence? Or is it the result of unwavering dedication, perseverance and resilience accompanied by numerous failures along the way? How you answer these questions gives insight into how you perceive others and equally important, how you perceive yourself. It shows whether you hold a fixed mindset or embrace the transformative potential of a growth mindset.

In pursuing success and happiness in life, a growth mindset is an incredible thing to have. Remarkably, the human brain possesses an extraordinary capability that sets people apart from computers. While a laptop computer is built with predetermined specifications and receives periodic software updates, your brain can undergo both "software" and "hardware" updates. Through experiences, neural pathways form, become dormant, emerge anew and fade away, allowing your brain to adapt continuously.

When people acquire new knowledge, they forge fresh connections between neurons, rewiring their brains to accommodate unfamiliar circumstances. This rewiring process occurs daily, and more remarkably, you have the power to encourage and stimulate it actively. As renowned psychologist Carol Dweck stated, "The hand you are dealt is just the starting point for development." This chapter delves into the captivating concept of neuroplasticity and its profound potential for transformation. It discusses the techniques and strategies you can employ to nurture and cultivate a growth mindset, empowering you to unlock your full potential and embrace a life of limitless possibilities.

UNDERSTANDING NEUROPLASTICITY

Neuroplasticity refers to the brain's capacity for change and adaptation. It encompasses the ability to reorganize, grow and modify neural networks, resulting in functional or structural changes. Contrary to the literal interpretation, "plasticity" refers to the brain's malleability rather than its composition. "Neuro" pertains to neurons, the fundamental units of the brain. Neuroplasticity allows these nerve cells to adjust and transform flexibly.

At its core, neuroplasticity represents the brain's ongoing growth and evolution in response to life experiences. It signifies the inherent capability to be molded, shaped or altered over time by generating new neurons and constructing novel networks. While scientists once believed that brain growth stopped after childhood, current research demonstrates that the brain maintains its potential for growth and change throughout an individual's lifespan. The brain can refine its architecture and redistribute functions across its different regions. Neuroplasticity manifests in various forms, reflecting the brain's incredible adaptability. With approximately 100 billion neurons and neural pathways comprising the human brain, neuroplasticity enables the reorganization of these pathways, the formation of new connections and astonishingly, the generation of new neurons.

The significance of neuroplasticity can't be overstated. It holds the key to breaking dysfunctional patterns of thinking and behavior while fostering the development of new mindsets, memories, skills and abilities. The implications are profound, offering a pathway to transformation and self-improvement. There are two primary types of neuroplasticity. Functional plasticity refers to the brain's ability to transfer functions from damaged to undamaged regions, compensating for impairments. Structural plasticity entails the brain's physical reshaping as a consequence of learning, allowing it to adapt its structure to optimize cognitive processes.

Neuroplasticity's workings become particularly evident during the critical developmental period of early childhood. The brain undergoes rapid growth during these formative years. At birth, each neuron in the cerebral cortex possesses around 2,500 synapses, the junctions between neurons where nerve impulses are transmitted. By age 3, this number escalates astonishingly to approximately 15,000 synapses per neuron. However, as people gain new experiences, the brain engages in synaptic pruning, a process where certain connections are reinforced while others are eliminated. This selective elimination allows the brain to refine and adapt to its ever-changing environment.

The benefits of neuroplasticity extend far and wide, enhancing cognitive capacities and enabling growth and recovery. By embracing neuroplasticity, influential leaders unlock their ability to learn new skills and knowledge and enhance existing cognitive capabilities. Furthermore, neuroplasticity strengthens areas where function has reduced and facilitates recovery from strokes and traumatic brain injuries, bolstering brain fitness and promoting overall well-being. It is a testament to the brain's remarkable potential for change and growth. By harnessing this transformative power, you can reshape your mind, expand your horizons and embark on a journey of continuous self-improvement.

Researchers have found that while the brain maintains plasticity through a lifetime, changes are predominant in specific environments and ages. For example, the brain changes greatly in the early years of life as it grows and organizes itself. Young brains generally are more responsive and sensitive to experiences than older brains. However, that doesn't mean adult brains can't adapt. It has also been found that neuroplasticity is ongoing due to memory formation and experiences. The brain never stops learning. Even after a stroke or instances of damage, healthy parts of the brain take over different functions to restore its abilities. How amazing is that?

As it turns out, regardless of your age, genetics or environment, there are things you can do to help your brain change and adapt. For starters, create a learning environment around you. These environments allow you to focus your attention, interact with new things and be challenged, all of which stimulate plasticity. This is especially critical for young brains but can give you rewards even in adulthood. If you can, learn a new language, read a different genre, play a new instrument, travel or create art — do what you can to enrich your environment. Your brain will thank you for it.

Secondly, make sure you are well rested. According to research, sleep is critical to the brain's dendritic growth. Dendrites are the small growths at the end of neurons that transmit information between neurons. By strengthening them, you encourage plasticity. Not only that, but sleep also affects your mental and physical health partly because of genetics and, in part, because of the brain's gray matter.

Thirdly, give yourself up to regular exercise and play. Regular physical activity prevents neuron loss in the hippocampus. Research shows that exercise also helps in neuron formation. According to a 2021 study, physical exercise boosts brain plasticity by improving functional connectivity. The U.S. Department of Health and Human Services recommends at least 150 minutes of moderate exercise per week. While you're at it, engage in play — take part in card, board or video games — and you will notice the positive impacts on your brain.

Lastly, practice mindfulness. Immerse yourself in the present moment and avoid worrying about the future or ruminating over the past. Awareness of the present — taking in the sensations, sounds and sights — is good for brain plasticity. Research has proven that mindfulness helps plasticity by strengthening neural connectivity.

As a leader, neuroplasticity helps you keep changing and adapting. With the right tools, you can reach levels of growth that exceed anything you previously imagined. The current body of research shows adult brains can rewire themselves with the right technique and some effort and persistence. In 2002, for example, Dr. Jeffrey Schwartz taught people with Obsessive Compulsive Disorder (OCD) to change their thoughts and responses to triggers by relabeling their compulsions and reattributing them to a hyperactive brain. As a result, his patients learned to act differently toward specific stimuli. In the same way, as a leader, you can rewire your brain to gain control over your habits and behaviors and reinforce a mode of being more consistent with your brand of leadership.

In the workplace, you can use neuroplasticity to your advantage as well. Research has proven that our brains are more malleable than we gave them credit for. With the right programs, practice and effort, it is possible to change how your employees and colleagues behave. Of course, this won't come quickly. It requires consistency and repetition to produce employees less limited by things like ability, aptitude and capability.

HOW MINDSET IMPACTS BRAIN PLASTICITY

How you perceive the world and yourself is intricately linked to your mindset. A mindset is a collection of beliefs that shape your thoughts, emotions and actions. It plays a pivotal role in determining your successes or setbacks, influencing your perception of personal potential. You can have either of two distinct mindsets — a fixed or a growth mindset.

Those with a fixed mindset believe abilities are fixed traits, unchangeable and immutable. They may attribute success solely to innate talent and intelligence, dismissing the role of effort and hard work. On the other hand, individuals embracing a growth mindset believe their talents and abilities can be nurtured and expanded over time through dedicated effort and perseverance. It is essential to note that a growth mindset does not imply that anyone can become a success by sheer will. Instead, it emphasizes the potential for continuous improvement and development in any chosen field.

A growth mindset revolves around the fundamental belief that inherent capabilities can be honed and enhanced through dedication and hard work. While this belief may not possess any magical qualities, it does catalyze action. Without a growth mindset, you may lack the motivation to invest the necessary effort and find yourself stuck in a rut. However, with a growth mindset, you can break free from those limitations and strive towards long-term goals whether in your professional life or personal relationships.

The disparities between fixed and growth mindsets extend beyond mere belief systems. They manifest in the level of invested efforts, responses to challenges and approaches to feedback and mistakes. Those with a fixed mindset may seek to delegate the most difficult parts, expending minimal effort when faced with demanding tasks. Conversely, individuals with a growth mindset recognize that achievement often requires exertion and regard effort as an integral part of their journey. Mastering new skills or concepts typically comes with substantial mental or physical energy and even repeated practice over time.

While those with a fixed mindset shy away from challenges and are driven by the fear of failure, people with a growth mindset view challenges as opportunities for growth and embrace them enthusiastically. They persevere and remain committed, knowing that valuable lessons await them on the other side. By conquering these challenges, they acquire mastery and move on to even greater accomplishments.

Mistakes present a significant divergence between the two mindsets as well. People with a fixed mindset may fear and avoid making mistakes due to potential embarrassment. They may shift blame to others or become defensive when faced with criticism. In contrast, those with a growth mindset perceive mistakes as valuable lessons, separating them from personal identity. Rather than taking criticism personally, they embrace it as an opportunity for growth and improvement. Being receptive to feedback allows them to enhance their performance in future challenges, underscoring how a growth mindset paves the way for success.

Your mindset profoundly influences your outlook on life and your ability to achieve your goals. By adopting a growth mindset, you embrace the transformative power of effort, view challenges as stepping stones and harness the wisdom hidden within mistakes. Cultivating a growth mindset empowers you to unlock your potential, break free from limitations and embrace a journey of continuous improvement and accomplishment. But how do you form a mindset in the first place?

According to research, there are two primary sources of mindset, praise and labels, which are most influential in childhood. One researcher found that children respond differently to various types of praise. Those who received personal recognition or were praised for their talents tended to have fixed mindsets. Such recognition sends the message that the child either has — or does not have — the specific ability or talent, and there is nothing to do to change it. On the other hand, children who received process praise —praise that emphasized their effort — tended to have a growth mindset. This praise teaches the youngster that the effort they put into a task counts. They grow up learning that success results from strategy and effort, both of which can be improved over time.

For example, if your child does well on a chemistry test, personal praise may be, "You are so good at chemistry." Process praise may be "I am impressed by your hard work." As a segue, you can take steps to ensure young ones develop a growth mindset by praising their efforts more than their results. That way, you focus on the process and teach them to be adults who trust in their hard work, effort and ability to create any outcome they desire.

The second source of mindset is labeling. Labels are characteristics assigned to people based on associations or stereotypes of groups. Labeling can either create a fixed or growth mindset. A person who believes girls are bad at physics can create a fixed mindset about females' abilities in that domain. Girls may grow up believing they are incapable of learning; boys may believe only males are good at the subject. Researchers found that when students checked boxes about race and sex, they invoked stereotypes that they had internalized and that affected how they performed in the next test.

So, what is your mindset? Do you have a growth or a fixed mindset? To help you know for sure, pick from the following statements that resonate most with you:

1. You are born with a level of intelligence that you can never change.
2. Regardless of who you are, you cannot do much to improve your personality and basic abilities.
3. A person can change who they are.
4. Someone can learn new things that enhance their intelligence.
5. You either have certain talents or you don't. You can't "just get" talent for writing, music, athletics or art.
6. You can develop new abilities and talents if you work hard, study and practice new skills..

You likely have a fixed mindset if you find that you most agree with the first, second and fifth statements.. If you resonate with the other remarks, you likely have a growth mindset.

That said, mindset affects your brain's neuroplasticity — how well you learn and adapt. People with a fixed mindset may be less likely to engage in challenging activities or take on new challenges, which can limit brain plasticity. This avoidance stems from their belief that abilities are fixed and can't be developed or improved. By avoiding challenges, they inadvertently limit their brains' plasticity. Neuroplasticity thrives on novelty, adversity and learning, all inherently present in taking on new challenges. By avoiding these opportunities, people with a fixed mindset deny their brains the opportunity to reorganize, grow and form new neural connections. Consequently, their potential for personal growth and development remains untapped, leading them to miss out on the transformative power of expanding their capabilities.

At the same time, people with a growth mindset tend to have increased brain plasticity. They embrace challenges and seek out new experiences, stimulating brain plasticity. Their belief in the malleability and development of abilities encourages them to actively pursue opportunities that push their boundaries. Engaging in challenging activities and exposing themselves to unfamiliar situations creates fertile ground for their brains to adapt and rewire. This constant exposure to novel experiences fosters the formation of new neural pathways, enhancing brain plasticity. As a result, individuals with a growth mindset expand their knowledge and skills and promote their brains' growth and development, unlocking their full potential for continuous learning and personal growth.

Adopting a growth mindset also can lead to physical changes in the brain, including a larger hippocampus and greater activation in the prefrontal cortex, which are all good for neuroplasticity. Neuroscientific research has revealed that the brain can reorganize its structure based on experiences and beliefs. When individuals with a growth mindset consistently challenge themselves, engage in learning and persistently work towards their goals, their brains respond by forming new connections between neurons and strengthening existing ones. The process of synaptic plasticity allows the brain to adapt and optimize its functioning. Additionally, the growth mindset encourages the release of neurotransmitters that promote neuronal growth and resilience. Over time, these physical changes in the brain lead to increased connectivity, improved cognitive abilities and a heightened capacity for learning and problem-solving. Thus, adopting a growth mindset transforms your attitude and lays the foundation for tangible and beneficial changes in your brain's structure and function.

LEADING WITH A GROWTH MINDSET

When it comes to predicting the success of a business, many factors may come to mind: market conditions, capital ventures or high-profile investors. However, the true determinant lies elsewhere. Irrespective of favorable circumstances, scaling a business into a thriving enterprise can be arduous without a crucial ingredient — a growth mindset. Behind the inter-working of any prosperous company, you will find an exceptional team leader who embraces a growth mindset. Experience has shown that the primary indicator of a successful company and effective leadership revolves around adopting a growth mindset.

Conversely, leaders who guide their organizations with a fixed mindset tend to foster a culture of fear. When challenges arise, which is inevitable, they interpret such situations as a failure and look for someone to blame. Since they believe personal growth and skill development are unachievable, they may even resort to demoting or terminating people they hold responsible. These leaders may sometimes feel compelled to solve problems or take on tasks alone since they lack trust in co-workers. Their fixed mindset often leads to stressful conditions that get in the way of business growth, creating a culture of fear where team members are afraid to take risks, innovate or voice their ideas for fear of being perceived as incompetent in the face of mistakes.

As a result, these leaders create demotivated teams that fail to reach their full potential or expand their capabilities. A fixed mindset leader's constant need to micromanage or "put out fires" often results in an overworked, burned-out and stressed workforce. The negative environment cultivates a defensive and blame-oriented culture where self-preservation precedes collaborative efforts to advance the company. In the worst cases, scaling up becomes nearly impossible. Even in the best cases, the growth path is marred by drama, negativity, miscommunication and stress.

Conversely, leaders with a growth mindset multiply their team's potential and foster a healthy culture of accountability that drives business growth. They see growth opportunities even in times of crisis. These leaders refuse to give into despair or seek scapegoats. Instead, they strive to accelerate their team's development and overcome any business challenges that arise. By leading with a growth mindset, they cultivate teams that engage in healthy disagreements, embrace feedback and set ambitious goals. Such groups are more likely to experiment, and companies with a culture of experimentation consistently outperform the broader market as evidenced by the Experimenter Index's impact on both tech and non-tech companies like Walmart, BBC, Sky UK, FedEx, and Petco.

The finest leaders continually develop their leadership skills and possess the qualities necessary to nurture a growth mindset within their employees. Admittedly, shifting from a fixed mentality to one of growth is no simple task. It requires a well-structured plan and the adoption of various business leadership styles. However, successfully incorporating a growth mindset can transform an organization into a thriving environment where employees flourish and feel fulfilled in their work. Ultimately, the power of a growth mindset lies in its ability to pave the way for unprecedented success in the business world.

Just think of people like Elon Musk, Sheryl Sandberg or Angela Duckworth and all they have achieved. Musk is known for his tenacity and willingness to take risks. The founder of Tesla, SpaceX and other tech companies often talks about learning from failure and being willing to change direction if necessary. This is the attitude of someone who sees failure as an opportunity to learn and improve, otherwise known as a growth mindset. Sandbag, the former COO of Facebook, encourages women not to let fear hold them back, a truth she ties to her incredible success. This also is a growth mindset. Duckworth exemplifies the same attitude in her determination to succeed described in her best-selling book "Grit." She makes a case for persistence, a factor in a growth mindset.

While a list of similar examples goes on and on, they reinforce the same point: A growth mindset makes you a lifetime learner. It encourages you to be open to new perspectives and ideas and be willing to learn from your mistakes. It keeps you adaptable and agile, keeping you and your team competitive despite any challenges. Not only that, but a growth mindset promotes persistence and resilience. You are better able to bounce back from challenges and stay motivated even in challenging situations.

Leaders with a growth mindset are more likely to be creative and innovative because they are willing to try new things and take risks. This willingness to risk-take helps them create novel solutions to old and new problems, inspiring their teams to do the same. They develop stronger relationships with their team members because they can take feedback and provide constructive criticism. Of course, this drives team engagement and performance up, proving that a growth mindset is an investment that is always paying off.

CULTIVATING A GROWTH MINDSET

If a growth mindset is such a valuable asset for authentic leadership, how do you cultivate it? Here are some helpful strategies:

- **Embrace imperfection.**

Imperfections are what make you distinct and extraordinary. By acknowledging and embracing your flaws, you celebrate your uniqueness. Rather than striving for an unattainable ideal, individuals should embrace imperfections as an essential part of their identity. Self-love flourishes when they recognize that flaws contribute to the rich tapestry of who they are as individuals. When you stop thinking you are perfect, you strive to be better.

- **Reframe challenges.**

When faced with daunting challenges, it is crucial to reframe them as opportunities. By shifting your perspective, you transform fear into excitement and view each challenge as a new adventure. Exploring different tactics and approaches allows you to navigate uncharted paths, develop new skills and interact with diverse groups of people. By embracing challenges as opportunities, you uncover hidden abilities and untapped potential within yourself.

- **Celebrate progress and growth every day.**

Reflecting on your daily experiences is a powerful tool for personal growth. At the end of each day, take a moment to identify one achievement, no matter how small, that brings you closer to your goals or contributes to your development. By focusing on your growth rather than perceived limitations, you shift your mindset towards progress and build confidence in your abilities.

- **Watch your words and thoughts.**

Attention to your words and thoughts is vital for nurturing a growth mindset. When you become aware of your internal dialogue, you can replace negative thoughts with positive ones. Practicing self-censorship allows you to guide your thoughts and cultivate a mindset of acceptance, compassion and personal integrity. Your words and beliefs shape your actions and outcomes, making it wise to choose them wisely.

- **Seek internal validation.**

Seeking approval from others can be a hindrance to personal growth. Often rooted in conditional love and past experiences, this approval-seeking behavior can lead you astray from your actual goals and hinder self-discovery. By cultivating self-acceptance and trusting yourself, you become comfortable with setbacks and failures inherent in your growth journey. Internal validation becomes your guiding light, empowering you to make authentic choices and embrace your unique path.

- **Celebrate others' successes.**

When those around you succeed, it is important to celebrate their achievements. Approach their success with curiosity, seeking to understand what contributed to those accomplishments. You can propel your personal growth and development by learning from others' triumphs and incorporating their strategies into your own life. Celebrating the success of others becomes a catalyst for your own growth.

- **Redefine "genius."**

Each person has a unique set of strengths and weaknesses. Appreciating and nurturing your strengths while actively working to improve weaknesses is the essence of personal growth. By redefining the concept of genius, individuals shift their focus from an innate and fixed mindset to continuous improvement. Embracing your areas of growth allows you to tap into your full potential and cultivate a growth mindset that fuels personal development.

- **Price the process.**

A lot of times, an obsession with the result keeps you stuck in a fixed mindset. One way to shift into a growth mindset is to remind yourself that the process matters more than the outcome. It is more about the journey than the destination.

- **Change how you describe your shortcomings.**

It is one thing to say, "I am not good at managing people," but it becomes a different matter when you add the word "yet." "I am not good at managing people yet" is more progressive. It shows that you hope to learn. It is more congruent with a growth mindset than the former. Get in the habit of adding "yet" to your shortcomings, especially when describing things you hope to learn.

- **Request constructive feedback.**

Growth mindset leaders are not afraid of criticism, especially when it is constructive. They know it is helpful for growth. Get in the habit of seeking feedback from those you trust to obtain helpful and honest feedback. Think of it as a chance to learn and develop skills that otherwise have been elusive.

- **Think of failure as a lesson.**

People with a fixed mindset tend to over-identify with failure. When they fail, they take it as a confirmation of an inherent inability. However, with a growth mindset, failure is just part of the process through which you learn. It is inevitably part of the process.

- **Appraise the effort and time required to learn realistically.**

Fixed mindset individuals shy away from challenges because they failed in the few and far-spaced times they've tried. They may have failed because they didn't put in the time and effort realistically required for the task. Learning a new skill and becoming good at it takes time. Remembering this can help you keep a growth mindset. You shift from focusing on the result to becoming more consumed with putting effort into the process regardless of how long it takes. Incidentally, this gets you closer to the end goal.

- **Own your attitude.**

If you know the value of a growth mindset, then make an effort and take the time to cultivate it. Persist even when it feels a bit difficult. Cultivate resilience. You are restructuring neural pathways.

A growth mindset is about continuous improvement. It embraces challenges and keeps you going when there are problems. It takes responsibility for your actions and recognizes that effort comes before mastery. The essence of a growth mindset for leaders is in the age-old saying that "practice makes perfect." Leaders who choose this mindset put in extra effort to make mental processes work for them, making them more likely to succeed in making the kind of life they want.

In the next chapter, we will consider how such a commitment to growth interacts with emotional processing and other elements to foster emotional intelligence.

3

LEAD WITH EMOTIONAL INTELLIGENCE

I f you desire to grow as a true leader, there is an emotional element to consider. It helps you successfully manage stress, coach teams, collaborate with others and deliver feedback. It is the element author Maya Angelou had in mind when she said, "People forget what you said and what you did but never forget how you made them feel." This element is emotional intelligence. Research shows that it accounts for close to 90% of what differentiates high-performing leaders from their peers with similar knowledge and technical skills.

As we know, emotions are complex. Researchers have classified them into only six basic emotions from which all others flow — happiness, disgust, fear, sadness, anger and surprise. It is said that other emotions build from these six. For example, jealousy comes from sadness or anger, while satisfaction is a form of happiness. It turns out that different brain parts, specifically within the limbic system, are associated with emotions. Emotions are experiences produced when certain parts of the brain are activated. This chapter deals with those parts and their concurrent emotions, defines emotional intelligence and helps you to develop it for effective leadership.

EMOTIONAL PROCESSING AND BEHAVIOR

Paul Ekman, a 1970s anthropologist, was the first to propose that people experience six basic emotions. Other scientists have since picked up that idea and expanded on it, while a few have disputed the number. Some researchers put the number at four; others identify as many as 27. As scientists research whether these emotions are universal, inborn or learned through experience, one thing is clear — emotions come from activity in different brain regions. The following list describes other brain regions involved in emotional processing:

- **Amygdala**

The amygdala primarily processes memories and emotions connected with strong emotions. It is a part of the limbic system responsible for processing fear and pleasure. It con to other brain structures allowing it to link to areas to process higher cognitive information. As a result, the amygdala organizes physiological responses based on available cognitive reactions.

An example of such a response is the flight-or-fight response. When stimulated by a perceived threat, the amygdala sends information to other brain parts to prepare to either run away or face the stimulus. Emotions like aggression, anger, anxiety and fear trigger this response. Generally, when you are stressed, the frontal lobes step in and override the amygdala and you respond rationally. However, the amygdala sometimes can act so strongly that it overrides the frontal lobes and you experience irrational over-reactive responses.

- **Prefrontal cortex**

The prefrontal cortex (PFC) helps to inhibit impulses. It is responsible for the working memory and includes planning. It is activated when you use emotional information to make choices. For example, someone may think about their feelings when they don't tell the truth. That prediction of emotion helps them not to lie again. A structure within the PFC triggers when someone anticipates how they will feel when rewarded. That area is activated by social approval, touch, smell and taste. When the PFC is damaged, a person may react wrongly because they can't anticipate emotions. Even though they know the consequences of their actions, they can't make choices based on how they will feel after their selection.

- **Hippocampus**

The hippocampus is involved in forming, organizing and storing new memories. It connects memories or certain sensations with emotions and enables recall. It is the hippocampus at work when a particular smell triggers a memory.

- **Insular cortex**

The insular cortex is activated when you are in love, crave a specific food, suffer a headache or listen to your heartbeat. As part of the cerebral cortex, it's involved in many functions ranging from sensory processing to representing emotions and feelings. The insular cortex has also been connected to motor control, risk prediction, bodily awareness, decision-making and other complex social functions such as empathy.

- **Cingulate cortex**

Early researchers thought the whole cingulate cortex played a role in emotion processing. Recent research has found that while different parts have a functional specialization, all tied to emotion. Scientists divide the cingulate cortex into anterior and posterior regions.

The anterior region is connected to other parts of the brain. It serves different functions, such as regulating the overall effect of emotion, assigning different emotions to external and internal stimuli and vocalizing different emotional states and desires. The posterior region, on the other hand, is activated by emotional stimuli, especially during memory recall. It is also active when people are daydreaming.

- **Periaqueductal gray**

The periaqueductal gray (PAG) is responsible for expressing behaviors that offer stereotyped responses. It modulates those responses and supplies the emotional tone to influence complex and aversive responses. Its primary function is modulating and regulating various physiological and behavioral responses, particularly pain perception and defensive behaviors.

PAG plays a crucial role in the descending pain control pathway, inhibiting or facilitating the transmission of pain signals. It acts as a central hub that receives and integrates those signals from different body areas. The PAG then communicates with other brain regions, such as the periventricular gray, rostral ventromedial medulla and spinal cord, to modulate pain transmission. It can signal pain-inhibitory pathways, releasing endogenous opioids and other neurotransmitters that dampen pain signals. This mechanism regulates pain sensitivity and the body's ability to cope with painful stimuli.

In addition to pain modulation, the PAG generates and controls defensive behaviors, particularly those related to fear and threat responses. It interacts with other brain regions, such as the amygdala and hypothalamus, to coordinate defensive reactions like freezing, fight or flight. The PAG's involvement helps ensure survival in potentially dangerous situations. It is also implicated in other functions, including sexual behavior and emotional processing. Its interconnection with multiple brain regions allows for integrating and coordinating different physiological and behavioral responses.

But how do your emotions influence your behavior? What is the relationship between emotions and how you act? Before answering this question, it is worth differentiating between an "emotion" and a "feeling," even though the words are often used interchangeably and are closely related. Emotion is not conscious. It is a physical reaction in the brain triggered by experiences, thoughts and memories. Feelings, on the other hand, are conscious. They happen in the mind as a reaction to an emotion based on how you perceive a situation or event. That is why individuals can be in the same situation and walk away with different feelings. Essentially, an emotion happens because of a physical response in the brain while a feeling occurs in response to that emotion.

Since emotions create and flow from a physical response in your mind, they can impact how you act. Imagine walking down the street at night and thinking someone may be following you. The thought creates fear, which initiates the body into the flight-or-fight response. You may then decide to walk faster or head to a safe place. If someone walking near you is not afraid, their behavior will be different. This kind of emotional influence on our actions happens all the time.

Your emotions not only affect your behavior, but your behavior affects your feelings as well. They have a bidirectional influence on your actions. Researchers looking at a group's expressions during a sports game found those who knew the outcome experienced different emotions as they watched it compared to those who didn't know how it would end. As individuals go about life, they see expressions of emotion within their context. When people interact, their reactions can influence how they interpret facial expressions. For example, if you wrinkle your nose at a fish market, it will be perceived differently from a wrinkled nose in a socially awkward situation. How context affects emotional interpretation is the same as how interpretation influences your understanding of the context that produced the emotion.

EMOTIONAL INTELLIGENCE

Have you ever encountered people who seem effortlessly composed during stressful deadlines, easily navigate awkward family gatherings and understand your thoughts without requiring extensive explanations? These people possess the remarkable skill set known as emotional intelligence.

Emotional intelligence, often called EI or EQ (emotional quotient), encompasses the ability to perceive, interpret, express, manage, evaluate and use emotions effectively and constructively to communicate and establish meaningful connections with others. It involves the ability to express and regulate your emotions and the capacity to comprehend, interpret and respond to the emotions of those around us. It is the art of self-discovery and applying that wisdom to navigate the outside world.

Coined in the 1990s, the term "emotional intelligence" gained popularity through the work of psychologist and author Daniel Goleman, who highlighted its significance in his book "Emotional Intelligence: Why It Can Matter More Than IQ." He identified five key components that contribute to emotional intelligence:

1. Self-awareness

Self-aware people recognize their behavioral patterns and motivations. They understand how their emotions and actions can positively or negatively influence those around them. Self-awareness helps them identify their feelings, label them and understand their origins. It involves recognizing personal triggers, acknowledging strengths and understanding limitations. A sense of humility or recognition of fallibility often accompanies self-awareness.

2. Self-regulation

Self-regulating individuals can respond to situations with emotional reactions that align with the circumstances. They demonstrate restraint when necessary and manage their impulses by considering potential consequences before reacting. They can ease tension, handle conflict, cope with challenging scenarios and adapt to environmental changes. Self-regulation involves harnessing an internal capacity to manage emotions effectively.

3. Motivation

Intrinsically motivated people have an innate drive for personal growth and development. Their pursuit of success is fueled by a genuine desire to evolve as individuals rather than being solely driven by external rewards such as money, fame or recognition. They find inspiration in accomplishing goals that contribute to their personal growth and fulfillment.

4. Empathy

Empathy involves striking a balance between self-interest and consideration for others. Empathic people understand and appreciate different perspectives, putting themselves in others' shoes. They draw upon their own life experiences to empathize with — and understand — the emotions of others, even if they haven't personally encountered the specific situation. They show compassion, withhold judgment and recognize that everyone is doing their best given their circumstances.

5. Social skills

People who have honed their social skills excel in collaborative environments. They are aware of others and their needs during conversations or conflict resolution. These individuals engage in open and welcoming communication by using active listening, maintaining eye contact, employing effective verbal skills and exhibiting open body language. They can establish rapport with others, adapt their communication style to suit different situations and demonstrate leadership qualities when required.

EMOTIONAL INTELLIGENCE AND LEADERSHIP

Emotional intelligence helps you be more flexible in your leadership. Developing EI competencies allows you to adapt to different leadership styles seamlessly. Research indicates that leaders who consistently demonstrate EI can deploy multiple leadership styles as needed to be effective. Leaders with limited EI competencies tend to rely on short-term styles, such as directive and pacesetting, which can create a negative climate. However, leaders with a broader range of competencies, thanks to emotional intelligence, are more inclined to utilize long-term styles like visionary, participative, coaching and affiliative.

Secondly, emotional intelligence helps you to optimize your leadership style. By developing specific emotional and social competencies, you optimize your style to align with desired outcomes. Research has found strong correlations between certain EI competencies and long-term leadership styles. Leaders who excel in competencies like conflict management, emotional self-awareness, inspirational leadership and empathy predominantly employ coaching, visionary, affiliative and participative leadership styles. Those with high empathy, teamwork and emotional self-control scores seldom rely on the directive style. Additionally, leaders with a positive outlook use the pacesetting technique judiciously.

Thirdly, EI strengthens employee performance. Emotionally intelligent leaders can create work climates that foster enhanced employee performance. Climate Index (CI) scores compare a workplace's current climate with the ideal environment that team members perceive. When reviewing CI scores for different organizations, researchers have found a positive correlation between scores and emotional and social competencies that reinforce long-term leadership styles. Leaders who excel in conflict management, inspirational leadership, empathy and emotional self-awareness are more likely to create positive work climates. Notably, leaders with low emotional self-awareness rarely achieved top-quartile climate rankings.

Fourthly, EI influences how your team members experience your leadership. Feedback from the Emotional and Social Competency Inventory (ESCI) sheds light on how different groups evaluate a leader's skills. The ESCI collects ratings from managers, team members, peers and others. Interestingly, team members' perceptions of their work climate and their leader's capabilities are often more discerning than their leader's superiors. Team members provide more positive or negative ratings of their leader's EI competencies based on their perception of the work climate.

Finally, EI helps you to improve team engagement. Developing emotional and social competencies directly impacts team engagement as evidenced by research. One survey provides insights into performance barriers and employees' sentiments about their organization. Its findings highlight the measurable influence of leaders on employee retention. While less than a quarter (22%) of employees plan to leave an organization within two years, this period extends with leaders who consistently demonstrate EI competencies. When leaders have at least three competencies, 42% of employees plan to stay at least five years. Notably, the key EI competencies that influence whether employers leave within two years versus staying for seven years address engagement, such as coaching and mentoring, conflict management, inspirational leadership, organizational awareness, achievement orientation, teamwork and empathy.

DEVELOPING EMOTIONAL INTELLIGENCE IN LEADERSHIP

For most people, emotional intelligence is a skillset that requires acquisition. With some effort and practice, you can develop or strengthen your EI in the following ways divided by different components.

Self-awareness

- **Keep a journal.**

To grow your self-awareness, set aside time each day to journal. It doesn't have to be lengthy — even 10 minutes will do. Use the time to reflect on your behavior in different interactions. Take note of anything that bothered you. Over time, you will have a record of your behaviors that you can use to study yourself from a distance.

- **Slow down.**

Each time you experience a strong emotion, such as anger, slow down and try to understand where it is coming from. Remember that regardless of the situation, you can always choose your response.

Self-regulation

- **Remind yourself of your values.**

Are you in touch with your values? Do you know the areas or things where you will not compromise? Spend some time becoming familiar with your ethical code. That way, when you must make an important choice or respond to something triggering, you will be guided by ethics more than emotions.

- **Stay accountable.**

When you self-regulate, you take responsibility for your feelings and actions. Commit to doing better if you're in the habit of blaming others when something goes awry. Admit your mistakes and deal with the consequences. You will find it easier to earn your team's respect.

- **Stay calm.**

How do you behave in challenging situations? Pay heed to your actions the next time you find yourself in one.. Take a deep breath to keep yourself calm. Notice any negative thoughts going through your mind and see how you react to them. Doing this more often will teach you to challenge your unwanted reactions and respond better to challenges.

Motivation

- **Remember your "why."**

Sometimes individuals lose sight of the reason they do their work. To help you stay positive, take some time to remind yourself of the important things about your career or your job. Remind yourself why you wanted to be where you are. Starting with your "why" helps you to re-energize and see your efforts with fresh eyes.

- **Keep hope alive.**

Motivated leaders stay optimistic regardless of what they are facing. However, that's a mindset that takes practice. Whenever you encounter a setback, practice identifying at least one good thing about it. Note it and keep it within view, no matter how small it is.

Empathy

- **Take a walk in their shoes.**

It's natural to support people who share your perspectives since they align with your experiences. However, it's crucial to try to understand situations from the viewpoint of others. Take the time to see things from different perspectives to grow your empathy.

- **Interpret non-verbal cues.**

Body language plays a significant role in communication. The ability to read and interpret body language can be an invaluable asset in a leadership position. Notice your body language and that of others when engaged in conversation. Crossing your arms, fidgeting with your feet or biting your lip may unconsciously convey negative emotions or disinterest. Correctly reading body language allows you to understand someone's true emotions better and respond appropriately.

- **Acknowledge emotions.**

Suppose you ask your assistant to work late and then sense disappointment in their voice. Take the opportunity to address their feelings directly. Express your appreciation for their willingness to put in extra hours and acknowledge a shared frustration about working late. Whenever possible, strive to mitigate future late nights to minimize the impact. For instance, consider offering them a morning off as a consolation. That is an example of acknowledging other people's emotions.

Social skills

- **Learn how to resolve conflict.**

As a leader, you will inevitably encounter conflict with a team member, a colleague or between people in your team. You may have to deal with dissatisfied customers or entitled vendors. Whatever the situation, conflict resolution will help you a great deal. Learn it.

- **Improve how you communicate.**

You may already believe yourself to be an excellent communicator and that is all good. However, there is always something more to learn. For example, you can learn how to give and receive feedback. You can learn how to send emails without flaming office gossip. You can learn what different jargon means in other circumstances.

- **Praise others whenever you can.**

You can use praise to inspire loyalty within your team. Ensure that you don't miss an opportunity to commend someone for their efforts. Learn how to recognize when work has been well done or a situation has been handled expertly, then make sure to praise it. In due time, it will improve team spirit and be well worth the work.

JOURNAL PROMPTS FOR SELF-AWARENESS

As a bonus, here are 10 journal prompts to guide your self-reflection and grow your self-awareness. Each is meant to help you understand your feelings, thoughts and behaviors as a leader. Below each prompt is an example of how it may be answered. Bear in mind that the examples here are short for easier reading. Yours can be as detailed as you like. Use one prompt a day or use the same one if you find it serving you well. Be honest in your self-appraisal; otherwise, it beats the point of the exercise.

1. Who inspires you as a leader? In what ways do you emulate them?

Example: *"I admire my grandmother's generosity toward us, especially when interpreting our actions. She always assumes the best. I look to assume the best of my team members whenever something goes wrong."*

2: How do you demonstrate respect for coworkers and team members? Do they show their respect in return?

Example: *"Whenever I have a complaint about someone's work, I speak with them in private first and allow them to do better. I see no reason to embarrass them in front of their team members. I have noticed that my team respects me for it."*

3: Reflect on times you acted poorly under pressure. Describe what happened before your reaction.

Example: *"During the board meeting, I rolled my eyes when discussing a difficult client. Before it was my time to speak, I was thinking about how they have made my team's life difficult, even when it was unnecessary. I should watch my thoughts next time."*

4: Did anything unusual happen at work? What did you learn from it and how does it influence future interactions?

Example: *"We hired a new CFO today. It turned out to be a former classmate who I had been kind to. It reminded me to always choose kindness unprovoked. You never know how it will pay out in the future."*

5: What have been the most rewarding moments of your job and career so far?

Example: *"I have cherished working with my mentee to grow her networks and develop her skills as a computer scientist. It is always a thrill to see her mastering a new skill."*

6: List some things you would want to hear from a leader.

Example: *"You are very good at managing your team. I love how punctual you are to meetings."*

7: What is your worst habit when collaborating with others?

Example: *"At the first sign of incompetence, I rush in and do their job because I do not like work that is done less than it should. This doesn't help team spirit; it doesn't help them to learn better; it certainly doesn't help me manage the work on my plate."*

8: What one thing about leading others have you picked up along the way and how do you use it?

Example: *"I have learned that you catch more flies with honey than vinegar. Whenever I can, before resorting to orders, I encourage my team members to perform by offering incentives."*

9: Identify two things you would never compromise on.

Example: *"My work-life balance and my integrity. I try to say what I mean and mean what I say. I also try to work when it's time to work, but leave the tasks in the office when I leave for the day."*

10: What do you feel most comfortable doing when managing conflict and why?

Example: *"During times of conflict, I've noticed I enjoy asking questions to understand the other person's perspective. It always helps me to assume the best about them."*

In this chapter, you have learned how important the brain is to emotional processing and management. You now know the different parts of the brain and how they influence emotion. You also know why EI makes you a better leader in improving employee engagement and performance, optimizing your leadership style and making you flexible in how you lead. You have found strategies for improving your emotional intelligence.

In the next chapter, you will learn to stay focused as you work toward your goals. You will see which brain areas are responsible for focused attention and how to optimize them to ensure success.

4

STAY FOCUSED

I f there was a magic key to accomplishment, it would be concentration. Success is the result of focused and well-directed energy. In time, you can become anything you long to be as long as your face is set in the direction of what you want and all your powers are brought to bear toward attaining it. That's the essence of this chapter. When your mental and physical resources are focused, you multiply your capacity to solve problems tremendously. On the other hand, when you do two things at once, you are doing neither well. Nothing adds more strength to your life and leadership than concentrating all your energies on set targets.

Have you ever noticed that the sun's rays t don't burn until they are brought into focus? Alexander Graham Bell discussed this idea, urging everyone to concentrate all their thoughts on work. William Matthews, an American journalist, had the same idea. He described concentration as the first law of success. Individuals must bend all their energies to one point and then go directly toward it without shifting their attention to the left or right. This is the kind of attention and focus you will learn in this chapter. It discusses the science of concentration and focus, the brain areas responsible for these functions and techniques to improve them.

THE SCIENCE OF ATTENTION AND FOCUS

Our human capacity for attention includes the remarkable ability to engage with specific information actively while disregarding irrelevant details. However, attention isn't an unlimited resource; it has limitations regarding capacity and duration. That is why it's necessary to effectively manage the attentional resources at your disposal to govern the world around you. In his renowned 1890 book, "The Principles of Psychology," psychologist and philosopher William James eloquently described attention as the process by which the mind seizes and focuses on a particular object or train of thought while potentially disregarding other simultaneous possibilities. This process involves selectively withdrawing from certain elements to engage with others effectively.

A good analogy for attention is that of a highlighter. Just as a highlighted section of text stands out and captures your focus while reading, attention directs your interest to specific areas or aspects of your surroundings. It is not merely about honing in on one thing, though. It also requires filtering out competing information and stimuli by tuning out irrelevant sensations, perceptions and data. Attention lets you allocate mental energy to information that holds significance in the present moment. Your attentional system enables you to concentrate on specific elements and also influences your perception of surrounding stimuli. It shapes the way you perceive and interpret the world.

Remarkably, attention is a fundamental aspect of human biology that traces back to the very beginning of life. Even newborns possess an innate capacity for attention. Their orienting reflexes guide them to determine which environmental events demand their focus, facilitating their survival instincts. For example, loud noises capture their attention. A gentle touch on the cheek triggers their rooting reflex, prompting them to turn their heads towards a source of nourishment. These orienting reflexes continue to serve us so that attention plays a pivotal role in almost every aspect of life, including education, work and relationships.

Attention empowers you to concentrate on relevant information, supporting the formation of memories. It allows you to navigate distractions and focus on and complete specific tasks.

Extensive research has delved into the intricacies of attention as researchers try to determine how many things we can attend to simultaneously and for how long. They have found that factors, such as our level of interest in a stimulus and the presence of distractions, significantly impact our ability to stay focused and on track. They have also recognized different types of attention, including:

- **Alternating attention**

This form of attention involves the skill of multitasking or effortlessly shifting focus between multiple tasks that demand different cognitive abilities. It does not include a simultaneous focus on multiple things but rather the ability to disengage from one task and seamlessly transition to the next.

- **Sustained attention**

Sustained attention, often termed concentration, encompasses the ability to maintain focus on a single task for an extended duration. During this period, individuals dedicate their attention to the task at hand and remain engaged in that behavior until its completion or a predetermined time limit. Recent studies indicate that sustained attention reaches its peak during a person's early 40s and gradually diminishes with age.

- **Selective attention**

Given that attention is a finite resource, we must discern what we give to it. Selective attention requires directing attention to a specific item in our environment and filtering out a vast array of other stimuli. It entails the capacity to deliberately choose and selectively attend to particular stimuli while disregarding others. For example, you might focus on a book you are reading while ignoring your neighbor's blaring car alarm. Selective attention is the ability to tune out extraneous external stimuli and internal distractions, such as thoughts and emotions, to maintain focus on the task at hand.

- **Limited attention**

Limited attention, also called divided attention, involves multitasking, much like alternating attention. However, in this case, attention is divided among several tasks simultaneously. Rather than shifting focus between tasks, individuals allocate attention to multiple stimuli concurrently and respond to various demands simultaneously. The misconception that attention is boundless has led many people to keep multitasking. However, research published in 2018 shed light on the limitations of multitasking, highlighting that our attention is, in fact, finite.

- **Focused attention**

Focused attention involves instantaneously responding to specific visual, auditory or tactile stimuli, such as a loud noise or a flash of light. It enables swift reaction to external stimuli, proving particularly valuable in situations that require immediate attention and quick action.

Have you ever felt frustrated reading the same paragraph multiple times without retaining its content? Or perhaps you've found yourself sitting in a classroom, facing the teacher, but completely lost in your thoughts? And who hasn't had moments of zoning out during a meeting, preoccupied with tasks on their ever-growing to-do list? These instances reflect the struggle with maintaining focus, the cognitive ability to direct your attention to a singular task and be fully immersed in it.

Focused attention is similar to entering a state of flow where you are fully engrossed in the task at hand and effortlessly filter out distractions. It allows you to remain undistracted by external stimuli and fully absorb yourself in the task at hand. You're focused on your attention when sitting at your desk and working diligently, undeterred by conversations happening around you in the office. You use focused attention when you attend a lecture and listen actively, resisting the temptation to observe those around you or doodle in a notebook. You use it when you watch a movie or TV show, immersing yourself in the storyline and resisting the urge to check your phone. It is focused attention that allows you to pursue a goal and prioritize it above distractions in your life.

Maintaining focus is crucial because it allows you to fully engage in a task without disentangling thoughts or shifting attention to other activities. However, it's important to note that while focus is valuable, excessive attention can be detrimental. When focus becomes hyper-focused to the point of tunnel vision, utterly oblivious to the world around you, it can hinder overall productivity and well-being. Striking a balance is critical to harnessing the power of focus without becoming overly absorbed to the detriment of other aspects of life.

It's worth noting that focus, concentration and attention are not synonymous, even if they are often used as if they were. Attention serves as your brain's illuminator, highlighting the vital aspects of your cognitive processes. Through your executive functions, your mind engages with various information sources, including sound, touch, smell and sight, as well as your inner thoughts and emotions. When you consciously "pay attention," you direct your focus toward a specific source of information. You might steer your attention toward the professor, absorbing their teachings in an academic setting. Alternatively, if you find the lecture uninteresting, you may divert your attention to classmates, social media or your thoughts.

On the other hand, concentration is the ability to direct your attention with purpose. It entails sifting through surrounding distractions and honing in on a singular stimulus that influences you. If you concentrate on something, your thoughts dwell deeply on it, engaging you in intense contemplation. For example, when you listen attentively to your professor, you focus on the knowledge imparted during the lesson. Your mental energy becomes devoted to the task of acquiring understanding and learning.

Finally, focus is intertwined with discipline and, to some extent, willpower. It involves deliberately selecting a specific focal point for your attention rather than yielding to external influences. You can adopt a narrow focus when working on a task, such as writing a work report, which requires profound concentration. Alternatively, you can adopt a broader focus by directing your attention towards overarching objectives, like furthering your studies while developing leadership skills.

Focus comes from intention while concentration is how you employ your intention. Focus is about your choice of where to direct your concentration. For example, you can consciously decide to concentrate on a spreadsheet rather than respond to emails. Concentration is about immersing yourself deeply into a task, such as being engrossed in the intricacies of a string of computer code. Focus entails prioritizing both minor and major goals, exerting all your efforts to achieve success. Concentration involves channeling your mental and physical energy towards specific tasks, ideally aligned with your objectives. Concentrating on studying for an exam necessitates focus to motivate yourself and concentration to triumph.

Focus determines what you filter out to distinguish the central point of your attention. You focus on your friend in the restaurant because their presence holds more significance than background music or crowd chatter. Concentration, however, determines what you think about. It entails processing your friend's words with greater depth than other stimuli in the restaurant. This suggests that it is possible to focus on a task without truly concentrating or vice versa. For example, you can focus on weightlifting at the gym by choosing to exercise. However, a work-related issue may linger in your mind, diverting your concentration from the immediate task.

Essentially, focus, concentration and attention engage different parts of your brain. Just think about it. Have you ever been in a situation where someone is talking to you but you don't hear them? You were probably on your phone. When you tried to defend yourself, you were met with skepticism. Researchers have found that the temporary state of deafness you experienced is genuine. In those moments, you genuinely did not perceive any auditory stimuli. This often happens due to your brain's selective focus, rendering you momentarily deaf or, in some instances, even blind. Observing how the brain prioritizes and directs attention towards certain stimuli while disregarding others is intriguing. That is probably because different brain parts are engaged in different circumstances. The following are the central brain regions involved in attention and focus:

- **Prefrontal cortex**

The prefrontal cortex facilitates the establishment and accomplishment of goals. It integrates inputs from different brain regions to process information and adapt accordingly. The prefrontal cortex actively contributes to a diverse range of executive functions, including directing attention towards specific targets, predicting outcomes of your actions, anticipating environmental events, controlling your impulses, managing emotional responses and planning for the future.

To show how these functions intertwine, let's consider a scenario where you are in a job interview. You know that you must concentrate on the interviewer while simultaneously retaining important details they mention. When confronted with a challenging question, you may feel nervous. However, you recognize that fleeing the situation will not secure the job. So, you suppress the instinctive flight impulse and instead seek clarification about the question. More information allows you to strategize and prepare your responses effectively, remembering the goal is to excel in the interview and secure the desired position. This is the prefrontal cortex at work.

- **Parietal cortex**

The parietal cortex plays a central role in directing attention to relevant environmental aspects acquired through visual, auditory, tactile, olfactory and gustatory senses. By collaborating with sensory processing regions of the brain, the parietal cortex selects and enhances behaviorally significant information, making it accessible to other brain areas for planning and executing physical movements.

- **Thalamus**

thalamus functions as the brain's information relay station. It receives and processes all inputs (except smell) from the body's senses before transmitting them to the cerebral cortex for interpretation. Additionally, the thalamus influences sleep, wakefulness, consciousness, learning and memory.

ATTENTION AND FOCUS IN LEADERSHIP

In the realm of leadership, focus and attention play a pivotal role in guiding and influencing others. A leader's field of attention — the particular issues and goals they concentrate on — serves as a silent directive for followers. Even without explicitly articulating it, leaders can shape the focus of those who look up to them. People choose where to direct their attention based on their perception of what matters to their leaders. This ripple effect amplifies the responsibility of leaders as they are not only responsible for their own attention but also bear the weight of guiding their teams' attention.

A fundamental way in which attention and focus benefit leaders is by helping them prioritize tasks. By honing their ability to focus, leaders can distinguish between crucial and peripheral responsibilities, ensuring the most important ones receive appropriate attention. This capacity to prioritize tasks allows leaders to stay on track and avoid distractions, leading to more efficient and effective task completion.

Furthermore, attention and focus significantly improve decision-making, a critical aspect of leadership. Leaders often face complex decisions that demand careful consideration and analysis. By directing their attention toward the pertinent information, they can evaluate the pros and cons, weigh various factors and make informed decisions. The ability to concentrate intensely and avoid cognitive overload enhances the quality of decision-making, enabling leaders to navigate intricate challenges with confidence and foresight.

Besides bettering decision-making, attention and focus also contribute to boosting productivity. Leaders who can maintain attention and focus are more likely to be productive. By eliminating distractions and staying immersed in their tasks, leaders can complete them more quickly and accurately. This heightened productivity benefits leaders and also sets a positive example for team members, inspiring them to follow suit and elevate productivity.

Effective communication is another area where attention and focus are crucial in leadership. Leaders who can focus on what their team members say demonstrate active listening, empathy and understanding. Concentrating on the conveyed message allows leaders to grasp their teams' needs, provide constructive feedback and build stronger relationships. By fostering an environment of open and attentive communication, leaders can inspire team members, encourage collaboration and enhance overall team performance.

Moreover, attention and focus contribute to increasing resilience in leaders. In the dynamic and ever-changing business world, they must stay focused on their goals while adapting to evolving circumstances. This resilience allows leaders to navigate the ups and downs, setbacks and challenges that inevitably arise. By maintaining their attention on the bigger picture and focusing on their objectives, leaders can weather storms, motivate their teams during uncertain times and emerge stronger from adversity.

Leaders who cultivate and master the art of attention and focus are likelier to lead with purpose, achieve success and inspire others to reach their full potential. Generally speaking, there are three categories of being a focused leader which leaders have to balance. They must navigate the fine line between focusing on themselves, others and the wider world. Neglecting any one of these areas can have detrimental consequences. Failing to pay enough attention to yourself could leave you unhinged, but excessive focus on others may give the impression of neediness. Meanwhile, a lack of outward focus can render you oblivious to the broader context.

- **Focusing on yourself**

Leaders must prioritize focusing on themselves. This is about self-awareness and recognizing the biases that may unconsciously influence decision-making. It is about being conscious of your internal judge, critic and censor and liberating yourself from their grip, which hinders effective leadership. Leaders accustomed to offering input rather than receiving and processing information may find this introspection hard. Still, it is necessary to filter out noise and fine-tune attention to what truly matters. It will require "cognitive control." It refers to the mind's capacity to process information and guide decisions and behavior in alignment with one's higher nature. It empowers leaders to stay focused on their goals despite emotional distractions. Those with reasonable cognitive control exhibit calmness during crises, keep anxiety in check and swiftly rebound from setbacks.

- **Focusing on others**

Leaders must also direct their attention to others. Those who prioritize understanding and connecting with subordinates and peers are highly regarded for the quality of their relationships. Regardless of rank, they lead through influence, inspiring the best in their teams and fostering cohesion.

To nurture relationships, you need two types of empathy. Cognitive empathy allows you to understand and appreciate others' perspectives, gaining insight into their thoughts, motivations and preferences. Emotional empathy enables you to feel and relate to others' emotions genuinely. This ability proves invaluable for coaching and mentoring teams, as well as providing exceptional customer service by intuitively grasping and addressing the needs of customers, vendors and third-parties.

- **Focusing on the wider world**

Leaders must not neglect the importance of focusing on the wider world. Visionary leaders excel in envisioning a future filled with opportunities. They possess the ability to connect present events with future outcomes and consequences. Influential leaders concentrate on two aspects of value creation. Firstly, they focus on "exploiting" existing conditions to generate future value. Secondly, they engage in the more challenging and adventurous task of "exploring" new avenues for growth. In an era where information is readily available, the true value lies in the leader's capacity to discern and prioritize the most pertinent information. This discernment enables leaders to formulate superior strategies and insights that set them apart.

TECHNIQUES TO IMPROVE ATTENTION AND FOCUS

If you have trouble setting priorities or struggle focusing, there are things you can do to up your chances. One reason why you may have trouble focusing is that you struggle to know what's important. In cases where you face endless tasks or a distant and vague goal, it can be hard to pinpoint what really matters. You may find yourself ticking things off your to-do list, multi-tasking but barely progressing toward your goal. Worse still, you could end up further from it, making you question the goal's value. Unable to know what tasks truly matter, the temptation is always to do what is easiest — or give up. To deal with this struggle, here are three strategies:

- **The Eisenhower Matrix**

The Eisenhower Matrix, also known as the Eisenhower Decision Matrix, is a time management tool that helps you prioritize tasks and efficiently use your time. Named after Dwight D. Eisenhower, the 34th U.S. president renowned for managing his time effectively, the matrix provides a simple, yet robust framework for categorizing tasks based on their urgency and importance.

Eisenhower used a similar method to organize his workload and make strategic decisions during his time in the Oval Office. As a former general and supreme commander of the Allied Forces during World War II, Eisenhower understood the importance of prioritization and the need to allocate resources wisely. He famously stated, "I have two kinds of problems: the urgent and the important. The urgent are not important, and the important are never urgent."

The Eisenhower Matrix comprises four quadrants, each representing a different category for tasks based on their urgency and importance:

- **Quadrant 1: Urgent and Important (Do First)**

Tasks in this quadrant are urgent and important, requiring immediate attention and action. They often have strict deadlines or significant consequences if not addressed promptly. These tasks should be given high priority and completed as soon as possible to avoid adverse outcomes or missed opportunities.

- **Quadrant 2: Not Urgent but Important (Schedule)**

These tasks are important but not necessarily urgent. They contribute to long-term goals, personal growth and strategic planning. It is crucial to allocate dedicated time for these tasks, schedule them accordingly and avoid procrastination. Quadrant 2 tasks often are neglected due to the allure of urgent matters, but investing time in this quadrant can prevent crises.

- **Quadrant 3: Urgent but Not Important (Delegate)**

Tasks in this quadrant are urgent but lack long-term significance or value. They often arise from interruptions, distractions or requests from others. While these tasks may require attention, they can be delegated to others, freeing up time for more important responsibilities. It is essential to assess whether these tasks align with your goals and if they can be handled efficiently by someone else.

- **Quadrant 4: Not Urgent and Not Important (Eliminate)**

These tasks have little to no urgency or importance. They are time-wasting activities, distractions or trivial matters that do not contribute to personal or professional growth. It is advisable to eliminate or minimize engagement with these tasks since they consume valuable time and energy that could be utilized better elsewhere.

To effectively use the Eisenhower Matrix, list everything you must do and then assess each task's urgency by considering deadlines, time constraints and potential delay consequences. Determine the importance of each task by aligning it with your long-term goals, values and desired outcomes and then place each task into the appropriate matrix quadrant based on urgency and importance. Once that is done, ensure you act accordingly per quadrant details. For example, prioritize action for the items under Quadrant 1 and schedule the ones in Quadrant 2. Using the Eisenhower matrix, you can gain clarity on your priorities, manage your time more effectively and allocate your energy to tasks that truly matter.

• **Warren Buffet's "2 list" strategy**

Warren Buffett, one of the most successful investors in the world, is known for his practical and disciplined approach to decision-making. His "2 list" strategy is a simple, yet effective technique to prioritize goals and achieve long-term success. The strategy involves following these steps:

- **Identify your top 25 goals.**

Make a list of your top 25 goals or aspirations. They can be various aspects of life, such as personal, professional, financial or social goals. It's essential that your list is comprehensive and includes everything important to you.

- **Evaluate and prioritize.**

Once you have your list of 25 goals, take a closer look at each one and evaluate their significance. Consider the potential impact, alignment with your values, and the level of commitment required for each goal. Then, carefully prioritize them based on their importance and potential long-term implications.

- **Separate your top five goals.**

From the prioritized list, identify the top five goals that are most important to you. You should focus on these goals and dedicate the majority of your time and resources to them.

- **Make an "avoid-at-all-cost" list.**

The next step in Buffett's strategy is to create an "avoid-at-all-cost" list. This comprises the remaining 20 goals that didn't reach the top five list. Buffett advises that these goals should be treated as distractions and avoided at all costs until the top five are adequately addressed and accomplished.

The core principle behind Buffett's "2 list" strategy is to maintain a laser-like focus on the most important goals while actively avoiding the lesser ones. Limiting your attention and resources to a few objectives increases the odds of achieving significant progress and avoiding the pitfalls of spreading yourself too thin. It's worth noting that Buffett's "2 list" strategy is a personal approach he employs and its application may vary from person to person. Nevertheless, the underlying principles of prioritization, focus and avoiding distractions remain valuable lessons for anyone seeking to achieve their goals.

- **Ivy Lee Method**

The Ivy Lee Method is a time-tested productivity technique developed by Ivy Lee, a prominent productivity consultant in the early 20th century. It's based on a straightforward principle: Prioritize your tasks and focus on the most important ones to maximize productivity and achieve desired outcomes. The method's simplicity and effectiveness have made it enduringly popular among leaders seeking to improve their time management skills. Here's how the Ivy Lee Method works and can be combined with other strategies for optimal task prioritization:

- **List your six most important tasks.**

Before the end of your workday, write down the six most important tasks you need to accomplish the next day. Limiting it to six ensures a manageable workload and prevents overwhelming yourself with an extensive task list.

- **Prioritize those tasks by importance.**

Once you have your list of six tasks, prioritize them based on their importance. Consider each task's impact on your long-term goals and the outcomes you wish to achieve. This step helps you identify the tasks that require immediate attention and those that can be addressed later.

You can use the Eisenhower Matrix for prioritization. Assess each task's urgency and importance, placing it in the appropriate matrix quadrant as described in an earlier section. Combining the Ivy Lee Method with the Eisenhower Matrixgives you a comprehensive framework for determining which tasks require immediate attention, scheduling or delegation.

You can also prioritize by evaluating value vs. effort. Think about each task's value and required effort. Some may have a high value and be relatively easy to complete, making them ideal candidates for prioritization. Others may require significant effort but offer limited value, suggesting they may not be the best use of your time. Balancing value and effort helps you allocate your resources efficiently.

You also can implement the "1-3-5 rule" to help you prioritize. Choose one big task (a significant priority), three medium tasks (moderate priorities) and five small tasks (minor priorities) to tackle throughout the day. This approach ensures you focus on a mix of important tasks while still accomplishing smaller, more manageable tasks.

The Ivy Lee Method's success lies in its simplicity, emphasis on prioritization and commitment to focused execution. Limiting your daily task list to a manageable number, prioritizing based on importance and urgency, and aligning your efforts with your long-term goals can enhance your productivity and achieve greater success in your personal and professional endeavors. Make sure to work on your list in order and move any unfinished tasks to tomorrow's list.

Emotion-Run Postponing

Often, focus suffers because of a tendency to procrastinate driven by a desire to avoid discomfort. Deep down, we know we can tackle the task at hand. After all, we've proven our ability to meet tight deadlines before. The real issue lies in the emotional triggers that push us away from discomfort. Without effective strategies to manage these triggers, we often starts tasks only when the discomfort of not doing them outweighs the benefit of procrastination. To deal with this, consider the following strategies:

- **Create a mental parking lot.**

Creating a mental parking lot means acknowledging the emotional discomfort associated with a particular task and consciously setting it aside for a designated time. This technique allows you to temporarily "park" your emotions and focus on the task without being overwhelmed by negative feelings. By creating this mental separation, you allow yourself an opportunity to approach the task with a more precise and rational mindset.

- **Begin single-tasking.**

Single-tasking means giving your full attention to one task at a time. Instead of attempting to juggle multiple tasks, which can lead to decreased productivity and increased stress, single-tasking allows you to concentrate fully on the task at hand. By focusing on one task at a time, you give it your undivided attention, leading to improved efficiency and quality of work. This approach also helps reduce the emotional burden associated with multitasking, letting you prioritize and complete tasks in a more controlled, mindful manner.

- **Just get started.**

Sometimes the most challenging part of overcoming emotional procrastination is simply getting started. The anticipation of discomfort and negative emotions associated with a task can prevent you from taking the first step. However, that initial action, no matter how small, can create momentum and diminish the emotional barriers that hinder progress. By focusing on getting started rather than the entire scope of the task, you overcome the inertia of procrastination and build momentum for completion. Breaking the task into smaller, manageable steps makes it feel less overwhelming and increases the likelihood of taking that crucial first action.

Lack of Drive

If you have left a trail of unfinished projects, you're not alone. A lack of motivation can strike when it's time to focus, leading to procrastination or preventing you from staying focused until the task is done. The human brain is wired to seek immediate rewards, making it challenging to stay motivated throughout projects that require days, weeks or even months to complete. This is especially true for tasks like planning and practicing that may not bring immediate external validation. It becomes difficult to gauge your progress and stay on track without regular feedback. You can suppress a lack of motivation with the following strategies:

- **Track your results.**

Tracking your progress and results involves recording everything you do, no matter how small. By visually checking your achievements, you can stay motivated by recognizing your progress. You can track results using a journal, spreadsheet or dedicated apps. Celebrating milestones along the way can further reinforce your motivation and keep you focused on your goals.

- **Recognize your biological rhythms.**

Everyone has natural patterns of energy and alertness throughout the day. By identifying your peak productivity periods, you can schedule your most demanding or essential tasks. For example, if you're a morning person, tackle challenging projects early in the day when your energy and focus are at their highest. Conversely, if you tend to be more alert in the evening, plan your activities accordingly. Aligning your tasks with your natural rhythm can make them less daunting and increase your motivation.

- **Use a timer.**

Setting a timer can be an effective way to combat a lack of motivation and improve focus. Divide your tasks by how much time they require and set a timer to alert you when time blocks end. Take a short break to recharge after each time block.

Excessive Multitasking

Multitasking often arises as a response to feeling overwhelmed. Focusing on a single task is hard when your to-do list seems to rival the length of "War and Peace." The temptation to jump from one task to another, simultaneously working on spreadsheets while answering phone calls and emails, becomes irresistible. We deceive ourselves into thinking that a flurry of activity is equivalent to productivity. However, the reality is that constantly switching tasks incur mental switching costs, resulting in reduced efficiency and wasted time as you readjust your focus. You can combat multitasking using the following strategies:

- **Pomodoro technique**

The Pomodoro technique is a popular timing method that breaks work into intervals. Typically, you work cycles of 25 minutes with 5-minute breaks. After completing four cycles, you take a more extended break. This approach provides a structured framework, allowing you to work in short, manageable bursts. Knowing you have a fixed period to concentrate on a task can boost motivation and prevent distractions. The breaks act as rewards and allow you to recharge, keeping you engaged and motivated throughout the day.

- **Limit the number of open tabs.**

Having multiple tabs open on your computer or browser can be a significant distraction source that encourages multitasking. Each tab represents a potential avenue for your attention to wander, making it harder to focus on the task at hand. By consciously limiting the number of open tabs, you minimize the temptation to switch between tasks or websites. Prioritize tabs directly related to your current task and close unnecessary ones. This way, you can maintain better concentration and prevent the mental strain caused by constantly switching contexts.

- **Turn off notifications.**

Notifications from various apps, social media platforms, emails and messaging services can disrupt your workflow and lead to frequent multitasking. Constant interruptions can break your concentration and make it challenging to remain productive. To combat this, consider turning off or silencing notifications during designated work periods. This allows you to create uninterrupted blocks of time when you can focus solely on the task without the constant urge to switch to different apps or respond to incoming messages. By proactively managing your notifications, you regain control over your attention and reduce the likelihood of engaging in multitasking behaviors.

Challenges in Time Management

As the American writer and educator Nir Eyal astutely states, "Time management is pain management." The way we structure our schedules, when done without intention, reflects a natural inclination to avoid discomfort. Instead of tackling the most challenging and high-priority task first thing in the morning when our minds are fresh, we often push it to later in the day when it frequently remains unfinished.

Another common struggle is accurately estimating the time needed for tasks, leading to frustration when unrealistic schedules go unmet. Additionally, leaving too many unstructured gaps in your day prevents you from utilizing goal-driven, top-down selective attention, forcing you to react to whatever stimuli demand immediate attention. To better manage your time, consider the following strategies:

- **Use to-do lists.**

A to-do list is a simple, yet effective tool for managing your tasks and prioritizing your workload. Start by listing all the tasks you need to accomplish, whether for the day, week or longer-term goals. Break down large tasks into smaller, actionable steps to make them more manageable. Prioritize your tasks based on urgency and importance. Consider using techniques like the Eisenhower Matrix (discussed earlier in this chapter) to help with prioritization. As you complete tasks, check them off your list. This provides a sense of accomplishment and motivates you to continue working through your list systematically.

- **Use time-blocking.**

Time-blocking involves scheduling specific time for different activities or tasks. It helps you allocate time more effectively and reduce the tendency to get distracted or overwhelmed. Start by identifying your most important tasks and assigning specific time slots to work on them. Be realistic with your time estimates and allow some buffer time for unexpected interruptions or delays. By dedicating specific periods for focused work, you create a structured routine that helps improve productivity and prevents multitasking. Use calendars or productivity apps to visualize and manage your time blocks effectively.

- **"Eat that frog."**

Popularized by motivational speaker Brian Tracy, this method suggests tackling the most challenging or undesirable task — the "frog" — first in the morning. Addressing the most daunting task early in the day gives you a sense of accomplishment and momentum that carries over to the rest of your tasks. This approach prevents procrastination and reduces the mental burden of the challenging task looming over you. Breaking the cycle of avoidance can significantly improve productivity and help you make progress on important projects.

Impact of Physical Health

The mind and body are intimately connected, yet physical health is often overlooked as a vital aspect of maintaining focus. Shockingly, one in three adults suffers from chronic sleep deprivation, disrupting communication between brain cells and impairing cognitive abilities. Irregular eating patterns or opting for light snacks instead of substantial meals are shown to negatively affect focus. Not only that, but many of us fail to drink adequate amounts of water, which can be detrimental to our ability to concentrate. It's no surprise that our bodies respond by sending internal signals demanding attention when these basic needs are neglected. To prevent physical health issues from stealing your focus, considering these strategies:

- **Drink water in the morning.**

Hydration plays a critical role in cognitive function. Starting your day by drinking water helps replenish your body after a night's sleep and boosts your overall hydration levels. Dehydration can lead to fatigue, concentration difficulties and decreased alertness. By starting your hydration in the morning, you enhance your brain's ability to function optimally throughout the day. Keep a water bottle nearby and make it a habit to drink regularly during the day to maintain hydration and support your focus and attention.

- **Eat healthy snacks.**

Proper nutrition is vital for maintaining optimal cognitive function. Eating healthy snacks during the day can help stabilize blood sugar levels, provide a steady energy supply and support brain health. Choose snacks rich in nutrients such as fruits, vegetables, nuts, seeds and whole grains. Avoid sugary or processed snacks that can cause energy crashes and impair focus. By fueling your body with nutritious snacks, you sustain your energy levels, enhance mental clarity and promote better focus and attention.

- **Move.**

Physical activity benefits both your body and mind. Regular exercise can improve blood flow, release endorphins and enhance overall brain function. Incorporating movement into your daily routine is critical for focus and overall well-being. Perform physical activity, such as walking, stretching or light exercises, to increase alertness, boost your mood and reduce feelings of fatigue. Be sure you take short breaks during the day to move your body.

Distractions

Distraction does not equate to a lack of focus. Instead, it refers to redirecting attention to something other than the task at hand. Distractions prolong the time required to complete projects, incurring mental switching costs (multitasking) as your brain constantly needs to readjust. Have you ever noticed how quickly you find something else to do when a project becomes challenging? Distractions are a temporary escape from discomfort, acting as pressure-release valves during a hectic day. It is important to note that concerns about distraction are not exclusive to today's digital age. Throughout history, people have struggled with distractions from televisions, radios, telephones and earlier technologies.

- **Eliminate everything that is not essential.**

Minimizing distractions starts by creating an environment conducive to focused work. Take a critical look at your surroundings and remove anything that isn't essential to the task at hand. Clear your physical workspace of clutter, unnecessary objects or visual stimuli that may divert your attention. Create a clean and organized environment that promotes concentration and minimizes distractions.

- **Know your priorities.**

Understanding your priorities helps you stay focused on what truly matters. Defining your short-term and long-term goals and identifying key tasks will contribute to their achievement. With a clear sense of direction, you can better allocate your time and energy to tasks that align with your priorities. When distractions arise, ask yourself if they align with your goals or if they can be postponed or delegated. This awareness helps you make conscious choices to stay on track and minimize the impact of distractions.

- **Avoid digital distractions.**

In today's digital age, it's easy to fall prey to digital distractions that can hinder productivity. However, proactive steps can help minimize them. Start by reducing or silencing notifications on your computer or cell phone during focused work periods. Consider using website blockers or productivity apps that limit access to distracting sites or apps. If possible, designate specific times for checking emails or engaging with social media to prevent constant interruptions. By consciously managing your digital environment, you create boundaries that reduce the temptation to engage in distracting online activities.

APPS THAT HELP YOU STAY FOCUSED

The internet has become a virtual workspace where productivity is easily compromised by endless distractions just a click away. While discipline plays a crucial role in staying focused, the reality is the odds are stacked against us. The internet has evolved into a dopamine slot machine meticulously designed by brilliant minds to maximize engagement. The goal is to keep us scrolling and "liking" posts, sites, etc., consuming every waking moment.

Attempting to combat this digital onslaught with sheer willpower alone is akin to bringing a water gun to a nuclear war. It's an uphill battle we're likely to lose. This is why we do well to use tools that help build discipline. This is where distraction-blocking software truly shines. These focus apps act as impenetrable barriers that prevent access to distracting elements. They are reminders that you've purposely installed the software to block distractions, nudging you back to your work. Paradoxically, it is liberating to be free from the constant pull of digital distractions.

App tools level the playing field and help you reclaim control of your attention. They provide a protective shield against the addictive allure of the internet, allowing you to focus on tasks without succumbing to the constant barrage of digital distractions. Depending on your specific needs and preferences, you can choose the app that aligns best with your workflow and desired level of distraction control. Experimenting with apps' various features and approaches can help find those most effective for you. Here are some apps that may meet your specific needs:

- **Freedom**

Freedom is a versatile app that allows you to block distractions across multiple devices simultaneously. It lets you create customized blocklists and schedules that prevent access to distracting websites, apps or notifications. By eliminating temptations, Freedom helps you stay focused and maintain productivity.

- **Cold Turkey**

This is another powerful distraction-blocking app that offers scheduled system-wide blocking. The blocker allows you to set specific time intervals when distracting websites or applications are inaccessible. Cold Turkey provides a more rigid approach to blocking distractions and can be effective for users who require strict control over online activities.

- **LeechBlock NG**

This browser-based app allows you to block specific websites or set time limits for accessing them. The browser extension offers customizable blocking configurations. It is particularly beneficial for those who struggle with internet-based distractions and want to limit access to specific websites.

- **RescueTime**

RescueTime is a time-tracking app that helps you analyze how you spend your time on various digital activities. It provides insights into your daily habits, tracks productivity and offers reports on how you allocate your time. It also includes a built-in website-blocking feature to limit your access to distracting websites based on your preferences.

- **Forest**

This unique app helps motivate users to stay focused and put their phones down. It uses a gamified approach, allowing you to plant virtual trees that grow while you work. If you leave the app or use your phone, the tree dies. Forest encourages users to resist using their phones, promoting greater focus and productivity.

- **SelfControl**

This distraction-blocking app is specifically for macOS. It offers a "nuclear option" by allowing you to create a custom blacklist of websites or apps that you want to block. Once activated, SelfControl prevents access to these blocked items for a designated period, even if you restart your computer or delete the app.

- **Focus**

Focus is an app that combines a Pomodoro (discussed earlier in this book) timer with distraction-blocking features. It helps you break work into manageable intervals, allowing you to focus for specific amounts of time and take regular breaks. The blocker feature prevents access to distracting websites during work sessions, enhancing your productivity.

- **PawBlock**

This app uses cute animal pictures to keep you focused. It allows you to create blocklists of websites or apps that you find distracting. When you attempt to access a blocked item, PawBlock displays adorable animal pictures instead, reminding you to stay on task.

Again, leadership begins with the brain. Leaders need to stay focused because their ability to concentrate and direct their attention on important tasks and goals is crucial for effective decision-making, strategic planning and leading teams. In this chapter, you learned that by maintaining focus, leaders can prioritize their time and resources, make informed choices and stay on track to achieve their objectives.

Distractions can derail progress, diminish productivity and hinder their ability to lead effectively. A focused leader sets a positive example for their team, maintains clarity amidst complexity and demonstrates discipline and commitment to organizational success. Staying focused allows leaders to navigate challenges, drive innovation, inspire their team and achieve desired outcomes.

The next chapter takes a deeper look at how the brain stores and retrieves memories, the process of learning and strategies to enhance memory and learning as well as their applications in leadership to help you better remember what matters.

5

ENHANCE MEMORY AND RETENTION

When you consider the statistics surrounding learning retention, the numbers can be quite alarming. Research on the forgetting curve reveals that learners tend to forget around 50% of presented information within just one hour. Within 24 hours, the number jumps to an average of 70% forgotten, and within a week, an astonishing 90% of newly acquired knowledge slips into oblivion. These figures raise essential questions about the effectiveness of training programs and the implementation of knowledge. How can we, as leaders, ensure the time and effort invested in training ourselves and our teams lead to tangible results if most of what is learned is lost over time?

To address this loss, it's crucial to consider learning retention when designing and delivering educational programs. We must take a step back and gain a deeper understanding of how learners acquire knowledge, how they retrieve it from memory and how we can leverage the science of learning to our advantage. Doing so maximizes the long-term impact of the things we learn and ensures we achieve our goals.

This chapter explores the fascinating world of memories and how they are stored and retrieved in the brain. It also looks at the intricate learning process and its connection to how the mind works. Here, you will uncover strategies to enhance memory and learning and apply them effectively in leadership roles. By understanding the mechanisms behind memory formation and retention, you can create more effective training programs and pave the way for long-term success.

THE PROCESS OF LEARNING AND THE BRAIN

Learning is a fundamental process that involves a lasting change in behavior resulting from experience. Many people associate learning with formal education during childhood and early adulthood, yet it extends far beyond the confines of the classroom and continues throughout life. The study of learning gained prominence in psychology during the early 20th century with the rise of behaviorism as a significant school of thought. Today, learning remains a central concept in various branches of psychology, including cognitive, educational, social and developmental psychology. Psychologists explore how learning occurs and also how social, emotional, cultural and biological factors influence this process.

Learning is an active process with multiple steps. When learning new knowledge or skills, we encounter information, pay attention to it, integrate it with our existing knowledge, store it in our memory and apply it in relevant contexts. For instance, if you want to fix a faulty toilet, you might search for a how-to video, watch it and use the instructions for the repair. Similarly, encountering an unfamiliar word while reading prompts you to look up its meaning, leading to acquiring a new word. While "active learning" often refers to interactive processes like hands-on experiments, it's essential to recognize that "passive learning" through reading, listening and observing is still a valid and effective form of learning.

A defining characteristic of learning is its capacity to generate lasting change. When you learn something, you retain the knowledge. When you see that new vocabulary word in another context, you know its meaning. Even if you need to refresh your memory by rewatching the video to fix a toilet next time, you possess the knowledge required to address the issue. Learning engenders enduring transformation and equips you to apply that knowledge in different situations.

Crucially, learning is a consequence of experience. It begins when we encounter a new encounter, whether reading a new word, receiving a concept explanation or attempting a new problem-solving approach. Through these experiences, we evaluate and determine the effectiveness of learned techniques or strategies. For example, by trying different methods for boiling eggs or exploring alternative routes to work, we assess their efficacy and subsequently incorporate successful approaches into future actions.

Ultimately, learning impacts attitudes, knowledge and behavior in positive and negative manifestations. It encompasses more than just "book learning." Learning enables us to acquire skills and shape our emotional responses to various stimuli. This inherent and continuous aspect of life influences development for better or worse.

As it turns out, the process through which we learn is not always the same. Psychologists have created different theories to explain how we learn. The first theory has to do with classical conditioning that happens through association. The physiologist who discovered this experimented on dogs' digestive systems and found that dogs naturally salivate when they see food. Eventually, they started to salivate when they saw the experimenter's lab coat. The dogs had learned through conditioning, by making associations, that the person represented a feeding soon. In this type of learning, an unconditioned stimulus automatically triggers a response until an association forms and a previously neutral stimulus becomes a conditioned stimulus.

Psychologists have also suggested learning through operant conditioning. Here, the theory is that we learn actions have consequences. According to psychologist B.F Skinner, classical conditioning explains some — but not all — types of learning. He suggested we learn lessons from actions that are reinforced or punished. With operant conditioning, a response to a behavior can lower or increase the likelihood of repeating the behavior in the future. Dog trainers routinely use this kind of learning when rewarding or scolding a pup when it behaves in specific ways.

Thirdly, we learn by observation. Psychologist Albert Bandura observed that watching others' actions and consequences is also a way we learn. In his experiments, children watched video clips of adults with an inflatable doll. Sometimes the adults ignored the doll but other times they hit it, yelled at it or kicked it. When the youngsters played with the doll later, those who saw adults abuse it did the same. They learned behavior through observation.

Finally, we learn through explicit — direct and structured — instruction. It is typically used in classrooms and involves feedback and opportunities to practice the learned lessons. Think about trying to follow a recipe that has a missing step. You may try to guess what comes next, but without explicit instructions, you may end up with a culinary disaster or give up on the recipe altogether.

Learning is not always a smooth process. It often requires over-coming various obstacles to acquire new knowledge and skills. They can present themselves in different forms, from environmental challenges to cognitive and motivational hurdles. For example, if you don't have access to necessary materials, your learning can be greatly impacted. If you can't find instructions or locate someone to ask about fixing that faulty toilet, you miss the opportunity to learn necessary repair skills. Similarly, whether in classrooms or workplaces, people may encounter physical, cultural or economic barriers that impede their ability to learn effectively. These challenges may limit access to resources, support or conducive learning conditions, making knowledge acquisition more difficult.

Cognitive factors also play a crucial role in the learning process and affect a person's learning ability. Factors, such as memory capacity and attention span, can either facilitate or hinder learning. Specific learning disabilities, such as dyslexia, can significantly impact how knowledge is processed, retained and accessed. Cognitive challenges require individuals to adopt alternative learning strategies and approaches to overcome limitations and achieve educational goals.

Finally, motivation influences the learning process. Both intrinsic and extrinsic motivation can significantly affect how much people learn. Intrinsic motivation refers to an internal drive to know for the sake of learning itself, while extrinsic motivation is driven by external rewards like praise or money.

Those with strong intrinsic motivation are naturally inclined to pursue knowledge and do not necessarily rely on external rewards, such as grades or prizes, to stay motivated. The level of intrinsic motivation can vary across different skills or subjects. Someone may require extrinsic motivators to complete math homework while being intrinsically motivated to research family history. Challenges with motivation can arise from various factors, including attention deficit hyperactivity disorder, depression and other mental health issues. Overcoming such difficulties often involves finding strategies to maintain focus, cultivating a sense of purpose and seeking support from others.

That said, different parts of the brain are involved in the learning process, including:

- **Hippocampus**

The hippocampus plays a critical role in forming and consolidating new memories. It is involved in encoding information from short-term memory to long-term memory. The hippocampus helps organize and link further information with existing knowledge, allowing for the creation of associations and the formation of coherent memories. It also plays a role in spatial memory and navigation, facilitating the ability to remember and navigate different environments.

- **Basal ganglia**

The basal ganglia are a group of structures deep within the brain that play a vital role in procedural learning and habit formation. They are involved in the acquisition, execution and reinforcement of motor skills and sequences of actions. The basal ganglia enable us to learn and perform tasks that become automatic with practice, such as riding a bicycle or playing a musical instrument.

- **Cerebellum**

The cerebellum is primarily associated with motor control and coordination. However, it also contributes to the learning process by playing a role in procedural learning and motor skill acquisition. The cerebellum helps refine movements, adjust motor control based on feedback and store procedural memories related to motor tasks. It is involved in acquiring and retaining skills that require precise timing and coordination, such as playing sports or typing on a keyboard.

- **Prefrontal cortex**

The prefrontal cortex involves higher-order cognitive functions, including working memory, attention, decision-making and planning. It plays a crucial role in executive functions essential for goal-directed learning. The prefrontal cortex helps monitor, evaluate and regulate learning strategies and behaviors, allowing us to set goals, make informed choices and adapt our learning strategies based on feedback and changing circumstances.

- **Amygdala**

The amygdala is involved in emotional processing and the formation of emotional memories. Emotions can play a significant role in learning by influencing attention, motivation and memory consolidation. The amygdala helps modulate emotional responses to stimuli and enhance — or inhibit — encoding and storing emotional memories. Emotionally salient events are often better remembered due to the amygdala's involvement in memory consolidation.

It is important to note that these brain structures do not work in isolation but interact with each other and other regions of the brain to support the learning process. They contribute to different aspects of learning, including the acquisition, consolidation, retrieval and adaptation of knowledge and skills. By understanding the roles these brain structures play, you gain insights into the neural mechanisms underlying learning so you can develop effective strategies to enhance learning outcomes.

HOW THE BRAIN STORES AND RETRIEVES MEMORIES

Memory refers to a person's ability to encode, store and retrieve information and experiences. It is the process by which knowledge and past events are retained and recalled. Memory allows us to learn from our experiences, navigate the world and build on previous knowledge. There are several types of memory, each serving different functions and operating within different time frames. The major types of memory include:

- **Short-term memory**

Short-term memory, also known as working memory, is the stage when information is temporarily held and actively processed. It has limited capacity and duration, typically ranging from a few seconds to a minute. This type of memory is responsible for maintaining information currently in use, such as a phone number or directions to a new location.

- **Long-term memory**

Long-term memory is the stage when information is stored for an extended period, potentially for a lifetime. It has a vast storage capacity and can hold a wide range of information, including facts, events and skills. Long-term memory includes the conscious and intentional recollection of information as well as the unconscious or automatic influence of past experiences on current behavior and performance.

Memory is a complex and multifaceted cognitive process, and the two types of memory interact and influence each other in various ways. The ability to encode, store and retrieve information is influenced by attention, emotional significance, repetition and the overall organization and meaning attributed to the data.

When you first encounter new information, encoding begins. Incoming information transforms into a neural representation stored in the brain. This process involves the engagement of several brain regions, including the hippocampus, prefrontal cortex and the medial temporal lobe. The hippocampus helps form associations with existing knowledge. The prefrontal cortex facilitates encoding by focusing on relevant details, organizing and categorizing information, while the medial temporal lobe processes and integrates the data before it reaches the hippocampus.

After encoding, the brain begins consolidation. This is the process by which memories become stable and long-lasting. Memories are gradually transferred from temporary storage sites like the hippocampus to more permanent storage in the neocortex. The neocortex, particularly its association areas, is responsible for the long-term storage of memories. Different regions of the neocortex specialize in different types of memory, such as the temporal lobes for declarative memory. As memories become consolidated, they rely more on the neocortex for retrieval.

You access stored information from memories through a process referred to as retrieval. When retrieving memories, multiple brain structures work in concert. The hippocampus helps reactivate stored memory traces and reinstate associated contextual details. The neocortex, which houses long-term memories, is responsible for the retrieval and reconstruction of information. Different cortical regions are activated depending on the retrieved memory type, such as the visual or auditory cortex for sensory memories. Emotional memories often activate the amygdala, enhancing memory retrieval and influencing the emotional content associated with retrieved memories. Finally, the prefrontal cortex helps the brain recover and monitor memories. It aids in the strategic search and selection of relevant information from memory and provides cognitive control during retrieval.

MEMORY AND LEARNING IN LEADERSHIP

The importance of memory and learning in leadership cannot be overstated. They enable leaders to make informed decisions, promote innovation, enhance communication, facilitate change management and increase resilience. Leaders often face complex and challenging choices. A good memory and the ability to learn let them draw on past experiences, lessons learned and accumulated knowledge. They can assess the potential outcomes of different decisions based on their memory of similar situations and then apply critical thinking to make informed choices. Memory and learning give leaders a broader perspective and a well-rounded understanding of the factors influencing their decisions.

Innovation is essential for staying ahead in today's rapidly evolving business landscape. Memory and learning allow leaders to tap into their knowledge and experiences to identify patterns, make connections and generate creative solutions. By drawing on their memory of successful or failed strategies, they foster a culture of innovation, encouraging their teams to take calculated risks and explore new approaches.

Learning and memory also boost communication. Effective communication is a cornerstone of leadership. With memory and learning, leaders can recall relevant information, key messages and organizational goals when communicating with their teams, stakeholders and customers. A good memory helps them remember names, details and important events, creating a sense of personal connection and demonstrating attentiveness. Furthermore, continuous learning helps leaders refine their communication skills, adapt their message to different audiences and stay up-to-date with evolving communication trends and technologies.

Leadership often involves navigating change and guiding organizations through transitions. Memory and learning play a crucial role in change management by enabling leaders to understand past successes and failures, identify potential challenges and develop effective strategies. Leaders with good memory can recall lessons learned from past change initiatives and apply that knowledge to improve future change efforts. Learning also allows them to stay abreast of emerging trends, new technologies and best practices in change management.

To cap it all, memory and learning help leaders build resilience by allowing them to reflect on past experiences and understand their strengths and weaknesses while learning from setbacks. Those with a growth mindset and who continually seek opportunities for learning and development are better equipped to handle adversity, bounce back from failures and adapt to changing circumstances.

STRATEGIES TO ENHANCE MEMORY AND LEARNING

You can apply the following strategies to improve memory and learning:

- **Structure and organize information and make associations.**

Breaking down information into smaller, manageable chunks and organizing it logically enhances understanding and retention. Create outlines, flowcharts or concept maps to visualize relationships between different pieces of information. While at it, make associations between the data and what you already know. Forming connections between new information and existing knowledge help in encoding and retrieval. Relate new concepts or facts to familiar ideas or experiences, creating meaningful associations that facilitate memory retrieval.

- **Use visual cues and mnemonics.**

Visual cues like diagrams, graphs or images can promote memory and understanding. The representations can simplify complex information, enhance recall and stimulate visual memory, which is often strong in many individuals. Mnemonics are memory aids that use associations or acronyms to help remember information. By creating memorable phrases, patterns or rhymes, you can encode information in a way that's easier to recall.

- **Write it down, recite it and rehearse.**

Taking notes by hand reinforces memory and understanding. Writing information in your own words engages active processing, helps to consolidate knowledge and allows for later review and reinforcement. Verbalizing information by explaining it to someone else or simply speaking it aloud reinforces memory. The act of articulating concepts or facts enhances encoding and strengthens memory traces. Rehearsing is about repetition. Repeating information aloud or mentally rehearsing it helps boost the memory. Repetition allows for the consolidation of information and increases the likelihood of recall.

- **Engage in active recall.**

Rather than passively reviewing materials, actively retrieve information from memory. Use flashcards, quizzes or practice tests to challenge yourself and reinforce learning through retrieval practice.

- **Get adequate sleep and exercise.**

Sleep plays a crucial role in memory consolidation. Aim for sufficient quality sleep to enhance memory retention and cognitive functioning. While you're at it, also aim to exercise. Physical activity is linked to improved cognitive function, including memory and learning. Engaging in regular aerobic exercise promotes brain health and enhances memory processes.

- **Train your brain to remember.**

Engage in activities that stimulate and challenge your cognitive abilities. Puzzles, crosswords, memory games or other brain-training exercises can help improve memory and mental performance.

- **Meditate.**

Practicing mindfulness meditation can improve focus, attention and working memory. Mindful exercises help reduce distractions and increase cognitive flexibility, improving learning and memory.

This chapter teaches you why remembering helps you as a leader. Memory and learning support informed decisions, promote innovation, enhance communication, facilitate change management and increase resilience. You know different brain areas play a role in memory encoding, storage and recall. You now have all the strategies to improve your learning ability and memory.

In the next chapter, you'll learn how to spark creativity and innovation. You can use recall to break barriers and create products and services that innovatively solve others' problems.

6

SPARK CREATIVITY AND INNOVATION

Did you know that recent studies have uncovered fascinating insights about creativity? Surveys conducted among 5,000 adults across the United States, United Kingdom, Germany, France and Japan have revealed some eye-opening beliefs about the role of creativity in economic growth and society. Approximately 80% of respondents emphasized the crucial connection between unlocking creativity and driving economic progress, while nearly 66% recognized the importance of creativity for the betterment of society. Astonishingly, only a quarter of the participants felt they were fully tapping into their creative potential.

This chapter delves into the multifaceted concept of creativity and innovation, explores the brain regions responsible for fostering creative thinking, examines techniques to enhance these cognitive processes and investigates their practical applications in leadership to help you be one of the exceptions.

UNDERSTANDING CREATIVITY

The concept of creativity is multifaceted and there exists no universally agreed-upon definition. While many standard definitions suggest that creativity involves solving problems or generating new ideas in unique ways, unraveling its complexities remains challenging. However, two key components frequently emerge — originality and functionality. For an idea to be considered creative, it must possess novelty extending beyond existing concepts. Additionally, it should demonstrate practicality or usefulness, rendering it more than a mere abstract notion.

Psychologist Mihaly Csikszentmihalyi identifies various contexts in which creativity manifests:

- Creative people often exude a sense of stimulation, intriguing others with their unique thoughts and perspectives.
- They can perceive the world through a fresh lens, unearthing insightful ideas and making personal discoveries. These creative revelations often remain known only to the individuals themselves.
- There are some who achieve creative greatness, leaving an indelible mark on the world. Inventors and artists like Thomas Edison and Pablo Picasso exemplify this category, contributing renowned and transformative creations.

Experts in the field recognize distinct types of creativity, as outlined by the "Four C" model. The first type, "Mini-C," encompasses personally meaningful ideas and insights known solely to the individual. It represents a subjective form of creativity. Next, "Little-C" creativity involves everyday problem-solving and adaptive thinking. This type of creativity helps people resolve daily challenges and adapt to changing environments. "Pro-C" creativity emerges among professionals who demonstrate creative prowess in their respective fields. Although they may not achieve worldwide recognition, their creativity is evident in their vocation or profession. Finally, "Big-C" creativity encompasses remarkable works and ideas that attain eminence in a particular domain. This form of creativity leads to revolutionary breakthroughs, be they medical innovations, technological advancements or artistic masterpieces.

Csikszentmihalyi proposed that creative people often possess a combination of traits that contribute to their innovative thinking. Among these critical traits is energy. Creative people tend to possess physical and mental vigor, but they also allocate considerable time to introspection and contemplation. Intelligence, too, plays a vital role as it provides the foundation for perceiving the world through fresh and even naive perspectives. While high intelligence is necessary, Csikszentmihalyi contended that not all highly intelligent individuals exhibit creativity. The ability to approach things in unconventional ways is paramount, but it helps if the creatively inclined person is also disciplined. That way, they can balance playfulness with a commitment to their work and passions, actively seeking inspiration rather than passively waiting for it to strike. Essentially, the creative process has the following steps:

- **Preparation**

The initial step in the creative process involves gathering knowledge, information and resources relevant to the task at hand. This stage is characterized by research, exploration and acquiring a deep understanding of the subject matter. It lays the foundation for creativity by building a rich repertoire of ideas, concepts and techniques. It involves immersing oneself in the topic, studying existing works and seeking inspiration from various sources. During this step, individuals actively absorb information and make connections between different concepts, thereby paving the way for the subsequent stages of creativity.

- **Incubation**

Once the groundwork is laid, the mind enters a period of incubation. This stage is characterized by stepping away from the conscious effort of actively working on the creative problem. It's a time for allowing ideas and information to simmer and percolate in the unconscious mind. Although it may appear that the person is taking a break from the task, their mind continues to process and integrate the acquired knowledge. It's believed that the subconscious mind works on the problem, making connections and generating insights that may not be immediately apparent. The incubation stage often involves engaging in activities unrelated to the task, allowing the mind to wander and explore new territories.

- **Illumination**

The illumination stage, often called the "Eureka moment," is the sudden flash of insight or emergence of a new idea. It is the breakthrough that brings forth a novel and creative solution. This moment of illumination can occur unexpectedly, seemingly out of the blue, or a specific event or thought may trigger it. It is a moment of clarity when pieces of the creative puzzle fall into place and a fresh perspective is gained. The illumination stage is often associated with a surge of excitement and enthusiasm as the creator realizes the potential of the new idea or solution.

- **Verification**

The final step of the creative process is verification. This involves evaluating and refining the new idea or solution. It's a time to test the creative concept's feasibility, effectiveness and practicality. Verification involves critically examining the idea, considering its potential strengths and limitations, then refining it through feedback and iteration. This stage may require experimentation, prototyping or seeking input from others to validate and enhance the creative outcome. Verification ensures the idea develops into a tangible and usable form ready for implementation or further refinement.

There is also a connection between creativity and personality. While the "Big Five" theory of character provides a framework for understanding personality dimensions, certain traits and characteristics stand out regarding creativity. According to the Big Five theory, personality is classified into five broad dimensions: openness, conscientiousness, extraversion, agreeableness and neuroticism. Each dimension represents a spectrum along which individuals fall, ranging from high to low or somewhere in between.

Among these dimensions, openness to experience emerges as a trait closely associated with creativity. Individuals who rank high on openness are willing to embrace new experiences and ideas. They possess a natural curiosity that drives them to seek novelty, explore uncharted territories, engage with diverse perspectives and experiment with fresh concepts. Such people thrive on the excitement of trying new things, whether venturing into unexplored realms, meeting new people or contemplating unconventional viewpoints.

While openness to experience is strongly linked to creativity, other personality traits and characteristics also contribute to the creative process. Intrinsic motivation plays a pivotal role as people who possess an inner drive and passion for their work are likelier to pursue new ideas and seek innovative solutions. Curiosity catalyzes people to question, explore and delve deeper into subjects of interest. This thirst for knowledge and understanding fuels creativity and promotes discovering unique perspectives and insights. Persistence also emerges as a crucial trait, enabling people to push the boundaries of their creative potential and persevere in the face of challenges and setbacks.

It's important to recognize that while certain personality traits are associated with creativity, it is not limited to specific personality types. The interplay between personality, individual experiences and contextual factors shapes the manifestation of creativity in diverse ways. Each person possesses a unique blend of traits and characteristics contributing to their creativity.

THE NEURAL SIDE OF CREATIVE THINKING

The brain's intricate workings during creative thinking provide a captivating glimpse into the neurological processes that underpin our creativity. While creativity is multifaceted, research has shed light on several key brain regions and structures that contribute to generating novel ideas and innovative solutions.

The prefrontal cortex occupies a central position in creative cognition. It is responsible for higher-order cognitive functions such as problem-solving, decision-making and flexible thinking. During creative tasks, this brain area engages in divergent thinking, which involves generating multiple and diverse solutions. It allows a person to break from conventional thought patterns and explore alternative perspectives and possibilities. The frontal cortex also facilitates cognitive control, enabling an individual to inhibit preconceived notions and overcome cognitive biases that may hinder creative thinking.

The hippocampus is also involved in creative thinking. It helps connect seemingly unrelated concepts, events and experiences, forming new associations that contribute to generating novel ideas. The hippocampus aids in mental simulation, enabling a person to manipulate information and imagine alternative scenarios mentally .

The basal ganglia, a group of interconnected structures deep within the brain, play a role in reward processing, motivation and generating spontaneous and novel ideas. They contribute to the selection and evaluation of ideas, filtering out irrelevant or impractical options to allow for the amplification of promising creative solutions. They also facilitate the coordination and execution of motor actions, enabling the translation of innovative ideas into tangible outcomes.

While brain regions are crucial, the white matter in the brain, composed of myelinated nerve fibers, forms the communication network to exchange information between different areas. White matter tracts, such as the corpus callosum, connect the left and right hemispheres, facilitating the integration of other cognitive processes. The efficient communication between brain regions supported by white matter enhances the flow of ideas, enabling the synthesis of information from various sources and fostering the emergence of innovative insights.

It is important to note that the creative thinking process involves complex interactions between these brain regions and with other areas not mentioned here. Furthermore, individual differences and unique neural architecture contribute to variations in creative thinking patterns.

There is also a connection between dopamine and creativity. Dopamine is involved in the brain's reward system, reinforcing behaviors associated with pleasure and motivation. It acts as a signaling molecule, transmitting messages between neurons and modulating various cognitive processes. Studies have shown that dopamine levels can impact creativity, influencing the brain's ability to generate innovative solutions and think outside the box.

One aspect of dopamine's influence on creativity is its impact on motivation and arousal. Dopamine enhances motivation and drive, promoting the pursuit of goals and the willingness to engage in creative endeavors. Optimal levels can increase the desire to explore new territories, take risks and persist in facing challenges — all essential components of the creative process. Conversely, low levels may lead to reduced motivation and diminished creative output.

Dopamine also appears to influence cognitive flexibility and the ability to make remote associations. Higher dopamine levels have been linked to enhanced cognitive flexibility, allowing a person to connect seemingly unrelated ideas, break away from rigid thought patterns and think in unconventional ways. This ability to make novel connections is a hallmark of creative thinking.

Interestingly, studies have also found an inverted U-shaped relationship between dopamine levels and creativity. This means that both excessively high and low dopamine levels can potentially hinder creative thinking. While optimal levels enhance motivation, cognitive flexibility and associative thinking, an imbalance can lead to hyperactivity, which may disrupt focus and coherence, or hypoactivity, which may dampen motivation and cognitive processes. It's worth noting that dopamine's impact on creativity is complex and can be influenced by various factors, including individual differences, task demands and environmental conditions. The interaction between dopamine and other neurotransmitters and brain regions further contributes to the intricate neural mechanisms underlying creativity.

If nothing else, these scientific facts about creativity debunk some myths people have about creativity. For starters, creativity is not reserved for a chosen few. This belief overlooks the fact that creativity exists within every person to varying degrees. While some may exhibit higher levels of creativity or possess a natural talent in specific areas, creativity isn't an inherent characteristic confined to a privileged few. Everyone has the potential to tap into their creative abilities and nurture them through exploration, practice and mindset.

Another prevalent myth suggests that creativity is solely a function of the brain's right hemisphere, while logical and analytical thinking reside in the left hemisphere. However, research has shown that creativity involves the dynamic interaction of multiple brain regions and networks across both hemispheres. Creative thinking draws from a combination of cognitive processes, including divergent and convergent thinking, imagination and associative memory. The collaboration and integration of various brain regions contribute to the complex and multifaceted nature of creativity.

Thirdly, contrary to the belief that creativity and intelligence are mutually exclusive, research indicates a positive correlation between the two. While traditional measures of intelligence, such as IQ tests, primarily assess analytical and logical thinking, creative thinking encompasses a broader spectrum of cognitive abilities. Creative people often demonstrate high cognitive flexibility, problem-solving skills and the capacity to think beyond conventional boundaries. Intelligence provides a foundation for creative thinking by facilitating the acquisition and integration of knowledge and harnessing them to generate innovative ideas and solutions.

Finally, the notion that mental illness, such as depression or bipolar disorder, fuels creative genius is simply wrong. While there may be instances when individuals with mental health conditions exhibit creative talents, it's essential to recognize that creativity is not exclusively linked to mental illness. The relationship between creativity and mental health is complex. While some people may draw inspiration from their experiences with mental illness, creative expression is not dependent on psychological distress. Many highly creative individuals lead fulfilling lives without experiencing mental health issues. We must avoid romanticizing or perpetuating the idea that mental illness is a prerequisite for creative achievement.

UNDERSTANDING INNOVATION

When the topic of innovation comes up, it often brings to mind images of flashy new gadgets and groundbreaking products, but innovation goes beyond physical items on store shelves. In the business world, innovation refers to the ability to conceive, develop, deliver and scale new products, services, processes and business models for customers. It goes beyond mere creativity and involves transforming ideas into tangible solutions that drive substantial net growth.

Research has shown that companies that effectively harness the power of innovation gain a significant performance edge over their competitors. In fact, mastering innovation can generate economic profits 2.4 times higher than that of other players in the market. While creativity is a necessary component, it is important to note that innovation itself leads to company inventions and growth.

Creativity is thinking in new ways and applying fresh perspectives to old problems. It's a critical skill in the business world, enabling leaders to adapt and develop unique approaches that may surpass traditional methods. Innovation takes creativity a step further by turning the spark of a new idea into a practical solution or process that provides value to others. It's the implementation or creation of something new that solves a problem or offers an advantage. Innovation is not limited to humans; various species demonstrate innovative behaviors. For example, birds and monkeys use tools like sticks to extract food from tight locations. This illustrates that innovation is possible for different species under different conditions and environments. It turns out that there are different types of innovation:

- **Business model innovation**

This type of innovation focuses on internal aspects of an organization, analyzing how it operates and generates revenue. Business model innovations often involve higher risks as they may require fundamental changes to the core decisions on which a business is built. They're best pursued when companies identify oversaturated markets, low customer satisfaction or outdated technology.

- **Product innovation**

Product innovations aim to improve existing goods or create entirely new products. They usually involve tangible items and are the most common form of creation. Examples of famous product innovations include smartphones, fidget spinners, wireless headphones and foot-massaging insoles.

- **Marketing innovation**

Marketing innovations involve creating new markets or increasing market share. They introduce new and positively disruptive ways for brands to engage with consumers. Marketing innovation can range from novel methods of communication to promoting existing products for alternative uses beyond their original intentions.

INNOVATIVE LEADERS

Researchers have identified certain traits consistently found among leaders considered to be innovative. These traits provide valuable insight into the characteristics and behaviors that foster a company's innovative culture.

Firstly, innovative leaders display excellent strategic vision. They possess the ability to vividly describe their vision of the future, inspiring their teams to work towards a common goal. These leaders provide a clear picture of the destination while empowering their employees to determine the path.

Secondly, a strong customer focus is a hallmark of innovative leaders. They develop a deep understanding of customers' needs and wants, constantly seeking to get inside their minds. These leaders actively network with clients and ask insightful questions, transforming what may be merely attractive to the customer into something fascinating. They're intent on creating a climate of reciprocal trust. They understand that innovation often involves taking risks and they establish warm and collaborative relationships with their team members. These leaders are highly accessible and their colleagues know they will support and protect them even in the face of failure or mistakes.

Innovative leaders demonstrate a fearless loyalty to doing what's right for the organization and the customer. They prioritize the greater good over personal agendas or pleasing higher-level executives. Their unwavering commitment to making decisions benefitting the project or company drives a culture of integrity and ethical conduct. This trait is supported by a culture that encourages upward communication. Innovative leaders recognize the best ideas often emerge from the lower levels of the organization and strive to create an environment that fosters open communication and idea-sharing. These leaders project optimism, energy and receptiveness to new ideas, creating an atmosphere of creativity and collaboration.

Innovative leaders also tend to be persuasive. They're highly effective in getting others to accept and embrace good ideas. Rather than imposing their thoughts onto their teams, they present ideas with enthusiasm and conviction, inspiring their colleagues to follow their lead willingly. They know how to set stretch goals for themselves and their team. These goals go beyond simply working harder and require finding new and innovative ways to achieve exceptional results. Innovative leaders encourage their teams to push beyond their comfort zones, stimulating creativity and ingenuity.

For innovative leaders, speed matters. They believe that quick action and experimentation are essential for progress. Rather than relying on lengthy studies or large committees, they encourage rapid prototyping and experimentation, recognizing that speed is crucial in staying ahead of the competition. They communicate these expectations honestly and candidly, providing straightforward feedback, even if sometimes blunt, to foster an environment of open and transparent communication. Subordinates feel confident they can rely on their leader for honest answers and insights.

Finally, innovative leaders inspire and motivate through action. They understand that for innovation to thrive, individuals must feel inspired and connected to a sense of purpose and meaning in their work. By demonstrating their passion and commitment, these leaders create a motivational environment that fuels creativity and drives innovation.

CREATIVITY AND INNOVATION IN LEADERSHIP

Leaders who embrace and foster creativity and innovation within their organizations are better positioned to drive growth, adapt to dynamic market conditions and cultivate engaged and motivated teams. Creativity and innovation serve as catalysts for organizational change and success. By encouraging a culture of creativity, leaders empower their teams to generate fresh ideas, explore new possibilities and develop innovative solutions to complex problems. Prioritizing creativity and innovation creates a foundation for continuous improvement and sustainable success. This proactive approach enables companies to stay ahead of the competition, identify emerging opportunities and adapt to ever-changing market dynamics.

Creative leaders also can inspire and motivate their teams in unique ways. They foster an environment that encourages and celebrates innovative thinking and empowers employees to share ideas and take calculated risks. By valuing and recognizing creativity, these leaders instill a sense of purpose and excitement within their teams, igniting a collective passion for achieving organizational goals. Such an environment cultivates higher levels of engagement, job satisfaction and a willingness to go above and beyond in pursuit of excellence.

Adaptability is crucial for sustained success in today's fast-paced and unpredictable business landscape. Creative leaders possess an agile mindset that embraces change and encourages experimentation. They proactively seek innovative approaches to address challenges and seize opportunities, enabling their organizations to through uncertainties with agility and resilience. By fostering a culture of innovation, leaders promote a learning mindset where failures are valuable lessons and stepping stones to growth and improvement.

Besides, creativity and innovation empower leaders to approach problem-solving and decision-making from fresh perspectives. Creative leaders are adept at thinking outside the box, challenging assumptions and exploring unconventional solutions. They encourage diverse thinking and collaborative problem-solving, leveraging the collective intelligence of their teams. By embracing creativity, leaders tap into a broader range of possibilities, enabling them to make informed and innovative decisions that drive organizational success.

TECHNIQUES TO STIMULATE CREATIVITY AND INNOVATION

Creativity is not a lightning bolt that strikes whenever it wishes and cannot be replicated. It is more like a muscle. There are things you can do to train your creative and innovative abilities, including the following:

- **Brainstorming**

Brainstorming is a powerful group creativity technique widely used to tackle specific problems and find innovative solutions. It involves gathering and recording new ideas in a free-flowing manner, typically in sessions led by a facilitator and attended by a small team of core members. While the concept of brainstorming has evolved, four fundamental principles serve as valuable guidelines when conducting brainstorming sessions.

The first principle is to prioritize quantity over quality. The idea behind this principle is that a high quantity of ideas will eventually lead to quality solutions. By encouraging a continuous flow of ideas without judgment or evaluation, the creative process can be fully explored, generating more diverse and potentially groundbreaking ideas. The second principle emphasizes withholding criticism during the idea generation phase. It is essential to create a safe and non-judgmental environment where team members feel free to express any ideas that come to mind. By temporarily setting aside feedback and critique, known as "blocking," individuals can contribute without fear of rejection, allowing for a more expansive range of ideas.

The third principle encourages the welcome reception of unconventional ideas. Innovative approaches can be discovered by encouraging team members to think outside the box and introduce far-fetched or unique concepts. These seemingly wild ideas can catalyze breakthrough solutions and provide fresh perspectives that might otherwise go unexplored. The fourth principle involves combining, refining and improving ideas. During the brainstorming process, ideas are built upon, connections are made between suggestions and novel insights emerge. This collaborative refinement allows for the progression and enhancement of initial ideas, ultimately leading to more effective problem-solving and creative outcomes.

Brainstorming offers many advantages for businesses and leaders seeking to enhance productivity and innovation. It creates a conducive environment for free thinking as participants share ideas without fear of judgment. This freedom fosters a sense of psychological safety, enabling team members to explore unconventional and potentially transformative ideas. Brainstorming also promotes open and ongoing collaboration. By bringing together diverse perspectives and harnessing collective intelligence, teams can pool their knowledge and experiences, leading to richer problem-solving and generating innovative ideas.

Brainstorming is the way to go if you want to generate many ideas fast. Participants can explore a wide range of possibilities by suspending judgment and allowing for a free flow of thoughts. These ideas can then be refined, combined and merged to form robust solutions. Additionally, brainstorming facilitates consensus-building. By involving multiple team members in the ideation process, decisions are reached collectively, ensuring a more comprehensive and well-informed path forward. It encourages a culture of continuous idea-sharing beyond structured sessions. Team members become more comfortable bouncing ideas off one another, fostering ongoing innovation and collaboration.

Thanks to brainstorming, you get access to fresh perspectives. It encourages out-of-the-box thinking and stimulates creative problem-solving. Breakthrough innovations can be discovered by challenging conventional wisdom and exploring unconventional ideas. You can also transform thoughts into actionable outcomes. By verbalizing and recording ideas, they become tangible and can be further expanded upon, refined and implemented. The icing on the cake is that brainstorming is an excellent team-building activity. As no one person owns the results, it fosters a sense of collective ownership and an inclusive team effort. You can use the following methods to brainstorm:

- **Brainwriting**

Here, the focus is on written contributions rather than verbal discussions. Have team members write down their ideas on a specific topic or problem. The thoughts are then shared and further developed within the group. This method allows for parallel idea generation, reduces potential biases and ensures equal participation.

- **5 Whys analysis**

This technique helps identify the root cause of a problem by asking "why" multiple times. It involves going deep into the underlying reasons behind a problem by repeatedly questioning the cause of each answer. By doing so, teams uncover the fundamental issues and generate creative solutions that address the core problem.

- **Starbursting**

Starbursting focuses on questions rather than answers. The team generates questions about a specific topic or idea, exploring various aspects such as who, what, when, where, why and how. This will help your team broaden its understanding of the topic, identify potential gaps and generate insights that can lead to innovative solutions.

- **Round robin**

Round robin is a structured brainstorming method where team members take turns contributing ideas individually. Each member can share their thoughts while others listen and build upon the ideas. This method ensures equal participation, encourages active listening and fosters collaboration among team members.

- **Reverse brainstorming**

Here, you flip the problem statement to focus on generating ideas for creating or exacerbating the problem instead of solving it. By identifying ways to make the situation worse, your teams gain insights into the underlying causes and generate innovative solutions that address those causes.

- **Rapid ideation**

This is a fast-paced brainstorming method that aims to generate a large number of ideas in a short time. It encourages participants to think quickly and spontaneously without over-analyzing or censoring their ideas. This method helps to stimulate creativity, explore a wide range of possibilities and foster a dynamic and energetic brainstorming session.

- **Mind-mapping**

A mind map is a dynamic tool that captures ideas and information through a unique blend of keywords, visuals and spatial awareness. Harnessing interconnected thought trains allows you to consolidate ideas in one comprehensive space. Mind maps employ branching pathways that emanate from a central concept, mirroring our natural thinking patterns. These branches provide pathways to bring up thoughts and information about specific topics. Have you ever experienced a surge of related thoughts after you have one brilliant idea? That's how mind maps work. They effectively capture this process, enabling you to nurture your creative ideas and prevent anything from fading into the recesses of memory. To create a mind map, you can use a mind mapping software like Xmind or Coggle:

1. Start with a basic idea. Identify the primary objective of your mind map and write it down. As the map expands outward from a central point, this main idea will become the focal topic of the diagram. Your basic idea could be a problem you are trying to solve, a project that is stuck or even a difficult subject you want to understand.

2. Add branches to the basic idea.

Once the main purpose of your mind map is determined, introduce branches that outline fundamental subtopics. These branches will help you to organize the information. You don't have to add many details at this stage; keywords and concise phrases will suffice.

3. Explore topics through additional branches.

After identifying the primary subjects within your topic, continue adding shapes until you exhaust valuable information. Ensure you maintain organization by placing more significant aspects closer to the central concept and more specific details in the outer regions.

4. Incorporate visuals and colors to customize.

Keep organization within your mind map by assigning standard colors to different levels of thoughts within the diagram. You can also add images to help you visualize and memorize various components of the mind map. They serve as connectors between shapes, deviating from the traditional box-shape approach.

Remember, the map's purpose is to visually represent the concepts and their relationships, making it easier for you to understand and remember them. Please note that the specific design and layout of the map will depend on your preferences and the capabilities of the mind-mapping tool you choose.

Here is an example of a mind map created with:

- **Analogical thinking**

Analogical thinking refers to the cognitive process of drawing connections and finding similarities between different concepts, situations or domains. It involves identifying and applying the underlying principles, relationships or patterns from one context to another. Analogical thinking enables you to transfer knowledge, insights and solutions from familiar or existing domains to new or unfamiliar ones. It plays a crucial role in creativity and innovation by fostering new ideas and problem-solving approaches.

It encourages you to look beyond the obvious and explore diverse perspectives. By linking unrelated concepts, it expands the conceptual space, allowing for the creation of innovative ideas and solutions. Analogical thinking also provides a rich source of inspiration. Drawing parallels between different domains allows you to apply successful strategies or approaches from one field to another, leading to novel insights and break-throughs.

Analogical thinking helps leverage knowledge and solutions from similar or analogous situations when you're problem-solving. Recognizing similarities between a current problem and a previously solved one lets you adapt and apply existing solutions to address the new challenge. Since the process involves using metaphors to explain complex concepts or phenomena, you get a fresh perspective that allows you to understand and communicate ideas innovatively, fostering creativity and conceptual understanding. To use analogical thinking, perform the following steps:

1. Clearly define the problem statement or area of opportunity you aim to address.
2. Have each team member individually research and find two inspiring examples related to the problem statement. The examples could be from other companies or industries.

3. In a collaborative session, have team members present their chosen examples to the group.

4. Collectively, facilitate the team to identify and select the three most inspiring examples from the presentations.

5. Create a template for each selected example, outlining the key elements that make it exceptional.

6. Next, apply the insights and lessons learned from these examples to your own company and industry.

- **Creative Visualization**

Creative visualization is a powerful technique that taps into the imagination to create vivid mental images of your desired future. According to renowned author Shakti Gawain, the process generally consists of four stages, each contributing to manifesting your desired outcomes. By adapting and embracing these stages, you can effectively harness the potential of creative visualization as a regular practice.

1. Setting goals

The initial step involves setting clear and achievable goals. When starting, it's beneficial to focus on goals you believe are attainable. Building upon small successes can gradually enhance your skills and confidence in creative visualization.

2. Forming the mental image

In this step, you create a detailed mental image of your desired outcome. Imagine the desired outcome as if it already exists in how you want it to be. Make the image vivid and immersive, incorporating specific details. See yourself actively engaging and enjoying the envisioned object, situation, or experience.

3. Returning to the image

Consistently revisit the mental image you crafted in step 2 as you go about your day. Gently bring your attention back to the image without feeling pressured to force its realization. Simply carry the idea with you as you go about your daily activities, reinforcing its presence in your consciousness.

4. Infusing positivity

In this final step, Gawain suggests infusing the mental image with positivity. Imagine the best possible outcome is unfolding in the present moment. Visualize the image with the belief that it is already happening, filling it with positive energy and intention.

There you have it. You need creativity and innovation to lead well. You need them to adapt to changing life and business circumstances and to grow your organization. In this chapter, you have learned what makes an innovative leader and have weighed yourself against those characteristics. You have interacted with ways to grow your creativity.

In the coming chapter, you will learn how to make the right call. When there are so many decisions to make and problems to solve, how do you know when you have made the right choice?

THE HALF-TIME PEP TALK

"Any man could, if he were so inclined, be the sculptor of his own brain."

— SANTIAGO RAMON Y CAJAL

In the introduction, you were invited to think of this book as your coach.

In any professional sport, every player is constantly looking to grow their skills and develop their game, and this is exactly what you want to do as a leader. The coach is there to facilitate that and help as many players as possible.

Sustained growth becomes possible when the whole team is working towards a common goal; in this case, that team is leaders everywhere. If we can change our approach to leadership across the board, we will create a culture of continuous learning and development, which will unlock our potential to make significant changes and take real strides as we lead our individual organizations.

So, during this half-time pep talk, you're invited to pave the way for other leaders.

By leaving a review of this book on Amazon, you'll show new readers the direction to take to achieve exceptional leadership.

Amazon.com/review/create-review?&asin=B0CLGTPV7F

Simply by discussing how this book has helped you and letting other leaders know what they'll find inside, you'll show them exactly where to look to find everything they need to become an excellent and ever-growing leader.

Thank you for your support. You're laying the foundations for a thriving community of outstanding leaders.

7

MAKE THE RIGHT CALL

We take pride in our ability to choose government leaders in the electoral process. We may not always be happy with our options on the ballot, but we enjoy the fundamental democratic right of choice. However, the ballot isn't the only place we make choices. As consumers in a free market economy, we have many options regarding services and products.

In fact, the sheer number of decisions we make daily is staggering. Just think about even the seemingly small choices we face every day. Which TV service should we subscribe to? Once it's set up, which channel do we want to watch? Do we opt for a regular coffee or a more elaborate concoction? What should we wear to work? Which route should we take to get there? Do we "like" a friend's post on Facebook? These are just a few examples, but they illustrate the countless choices we confront throughout the day.

Researchers at Cornell University recently worked to quantify the question of choice. Astonishingly, they estimate that we make about 226.7 daily decisions related to food alone. As our level of responsibility increases, so does the number of choices we must make. On average, it's estimated that adults make around 35,000 remotely conscious decisions each day. Each decision, regardless of its scale, carries with it a range of consequences, both positive and negative. We make choices using different strategies. Some are impulsive and swift, while others comply with what's popular, in authority or most comfortable. Some are delegated, while others are about avoidance. Other choices involve carefully weighing the options, prioritizing and reflecting on the most significant impact.

We employ a combination of decision-making strategies to cope with the sheer volume of choices that confront us daily. Interestingly, our decision-making strategy is the first choice in the process. As it is, the implications of this constant decision-making are significant. Our choices shape our lives, determining the paths we take and the outcomes we experience. They influence our relationships, careers and overall well-being. It is essential, therefore, to approach decision-making with mindfulness and consideration. This chapter discusses the cognitive process of decision-making and problem-solving, the brain regions involved, strategies to improve processes and their applications in leadership, all to help you make the best choices and use your time as best as possible.

UNDERSTANDING DECISION-MAKING AND PROBLEM-SOLVING

When we talk about decision-making, we're simply referring to the process of making a choice. Sounds easy, right? Well, not always. Decision-making can be downright complex, especially in an organizational context. Some people will go to great lengths —and even shell out serious cash — to avoid making decisions. Just think about Steve Jobs who limited his wardrobe to only black turtlenecks just to avoid the daily hassle of deciding what to wear. According to researchers at McKinsey, who were trying to understand how leaders spend their time, executives spend significant time — almost 40% on average — making decisions. But here's the kicker: Many believe that most of that time is poorly used. It's no wonder we struggle with decisions so much that we get exhausted from making too many choices. There is even a name for it: decision fatigue.

So, what exactly do we mean when we say someone has good decision-making skills? Those nifty abilities help us choose the best solutions to challenges. With these skills in our arsenal, we can make informed decisions by gathering all the relevant information and data and considering multiple perspectives. It's like having a superpower involving collaboration, analysis, leadership, intuition, reasoning, organization, etc.

When it comes to decision-making, collaboration is crucial. We can't just sit in a vacuum and expect to make the best choices. It's important to gather input from others, hear different viewpoints and weigh all the options. Analyzing the situation is also crucial. We must dig deep, examine the data and understand the potential consequences of each choice. Leadership comes into play as well. A good decision-maker knows how to take charge, rally the team and guide everyone toward the best course of action.

But it's not all about cold, hard facts. Intuition plays a role, too. Sometimes we just have to trust our gut instincts and do what feels right. Reasoning is another essential aspect of decision-making. We need to think logically, evaluate the pros and cons, then arrive at a sound judgment. And let's not forget about organization. Keeping track of all the information, deadlines and priorities is essential to making well-informed decisions.

Ultimately, good decision-making skills are like a finely tuned orchestra. They require a delicate balance of abilities and a willingness to embrace the process. It's not about making the perfect choice every time but making the best choice given the circumstances. So, the next time you face a tough decision, remember that decision-making is an art. It takes practice, patience and a willingness to learn from past successes and failures. With the right skills in your toolkit, you can navigate the complexities of decision-making like a pro. And who knows? You might just become the Steve Jobs of your life, with or without the black turtlenecks.

According to research, there are seven steps you can take for effective decision-making.

1. Clarify the decision.

First, you need to identify the decision at hand. Take a moment to really understand what it is that requires a decision from you. This clarity is crucial because it sets the stage for the entire process.

2. Gather the necessary information.

Once you've nailed down the nature of the decision, it's time to gather all the relevant information. This step requires a combination of internal and external efforts. Look inward and assess your values, priorities and how this decision aligns with your goals. Simultaneously, venture outward and seek information from various sources: the internet, books, other people and other relevant sources. Cast a wide net to ensure you comprehensively understand the situation.

3. Figure out your alternatives.

As you gather information, you'll likely come across various possible paths of action. You can let your imagination run wild and create new alternatives based on your acquired knowledge. This step is all about brainstorming and listing every possible and desirable option that comes to mind. Leave no stone unturned.

4. Envision the outcomes for each alternative.

After weighing the evidence and considering the alternatives, it's time to envision the outcomes. Draw upon the information you've gathered and your emotions to imagine what each option would be like if you pursued it to the end. Reflect on whether each choice would effectively meet or resolve the initial need that prompted your decision-making. As you navigate through this internal struggle, you'll naturally develop a preference for specific alternatives — ones that hold more promise in aligning with your goals.

5. Arrange the alternatives by priority and make your choice.

Once you've reached this point, it's time to prioritize the alternatives based on your value system. Then comes the moment of truth: Choose the alternative that appears to be the best fit for you. It's even possible to select a combination of other options if appropriate.

6. Put your choice into action.

After you've decided, it's time to put it into action. Take proactive steps to implement your choice but don't stop there.

7. Review and assess.

It's essential to review your decision and carefully assess its consequences. Always consider whether your chosen alternative has effectively addressed the identified need. If it hasn't met the purpose, retrace your steps in the decision-making process. This could involve gathering more detailed, slightly different information or exploring additional alternatives you may have missed initially. The goal is to make a new decision considering the lessons learned from the previous one.

In essence, decision-making is an iterative process. It involves evaluating, choosing, acting and reflecting. By following this cycle and being open to reassessment, you can refine your decision-making skills and increase your odds of making choices that truly fulfill your needs and aspirations.

We can't talk about decision-making without discussing problem-solving. While many people often use "problem-solving" and "decision-making" interchangeably, it's important to recognize they are distinct concepts. The fundamental difference between problem-solving and decision-making lies in their nature. Problem-solving is a process to identify and explore potential solutions for a given situation. In contrast, decision-making is based on insights gained throughout the problem-solving process.

Problem-solving entails an analytical approach in which people strive to uncover and evaluate possible solutions. It's a complex and multifaceted process that requires judgment calls and decision-making at different stages. In other words, decision-making is an integral part of the problem-solving journey as it involves choosing a course of action among the available options.

On the other hand, decision-making is the act of making choices based on personal judgment and evaluation. The ability to make sound decisions is especially crucial for leaders. As they solve problems, they often encounter numerous decisions that must be made along the way. Decision-making skills enable leaders to determine the most suitable solution and take the steps necessary to address the problem effectively. The skills associated with problem-solving include research, analysis, communication, decision-making and dependability.

Just like there is a process for effective decision-making, there is one for effective problem-solving. It involves four steps:

1. Start by defining the problem.

To truly address the problem, it's crucial to diagnose the situation and focus on its root causes rather than just the problem's symptoms. Effective problem-solving techniques include using flowcharts to map out the expected steps of a process and cause-and-effect diagrams to identify and analyze the underlying causes. Ensure you engage the relevant stakeholders, use factual information, compare expectations with reality and emphasize identifying the root causes of the problem.

2. Generate alternative solutions.

Evaluate their potential impact based on your envisioned "what should be" model — your idea of the ideal. Instead of immediately selecting one solution, it's beneficial to postpone the decision-making process and encourage the proposal of multiple alternatives. Considering a range of options significantly increases the chances of finding an ideal solution. Brainstorming and team problem-solving techniques are valuable tools during this phase.

It's important to generate numerous alternative solutions before conducting a final evaluation. A common mistake is to evaluate alternatives as they are presented and pick the first acceptable solution, even if it may not be the best fit. By focusing only on achieving desired results, you may miss the opportunity to discover new insights that can enhance problem-solving.

3. Evaluate and pick the best alternative.

Skilled problem-solvers consider various factors, such as the extent to which a particular alternative solves the problem without causing unforeseen issues, the acceptance of the choice by all involved parties, the likelihood of successful implementation and the compatibility of the option with organizational constraints.

4. Implement and follow up on the solution.

Leaders may be responsible for directing others to execute the solution, promoting its adoption or facilitating implementation with the assistance of others. Remember that involving stakeholders in the implementation process helps foster buy-in, support and minimizes resistance to subsequent changes.

Clearly, problem-solving and decision-making are distinct skills, which are significantly important in leadership. However, it's worth noting they also share some commonalities. Both rely on critical thinking, a process that involves questioning your assumptions and those of others. It is a foundation for determining the next steps to solve a problem effectively. Through critical thinking, a leader engages in research, analysis, questioning and exploration of new ideas. This approach allows for a comprehensive understanding of the situation, empowering the leader to make informed decisions not confined by subjective perspectives or status quo limitations.

THE NEUROSCIENCE OF CHOICE

Decision-making and problem-solving are intricate cognitive processes that require the collaboration of several brain regions. To be effective, these processes require a balance between logical thinking and emotional intelligence as emotions can influence our perceptions and responses to different situations. Brain regions that play a role in decision-making and problem-solving include:

- **Prefrontal cortex**

This region affects its executive functions such as planning, decision-making, problem-solving, self-control and prioritizing long-term goals. Damage to the prefrontal cortex can lead to difficulties in daily functioning, personality changes and abnormal emotional responses.

- **Anterior cingulate cortex (ACC)**

The ACC plays a crucial role in problem-solving. It identifies conflicts within the information the brain receives and sends them to the prefrontal cortex for resolution. Conflicts can arise in different contexts, including within oneself (Me vs. Me), within relationships (Me vs. Us) and between one's group and other groups (Me vs. Them). The ACC's role is to alert the prefrontal cortex to resolve these conflicts.

- **The insula**

The insula integrates emotional, cognitive and sensory-motor systems. It serves as a hub for various functions, including social cognition, empathy, reward-driven decision-making, arousal, reactivity to emotional stimuli and somatic pain processing. The insula's role is complex, ranging from processing sensorimotor sensations in the posterior insula to perceiving subjective emotions in the anterior insula. The insula interacts with other brain regions, such as the ventrolateral prefrontal cortex and the anterior cingulate cortex, to facilitate cognitive and emotional processes.

DECISION-MAKING AND PROBLEM-SOLVING IN LEADERSHIP

Effective decision-making and problem-solving skills play a vital role in leadership, contributing to the success and growth of organizations. They must navigate challenges and make choices that align with organizational objectives. Leaders who possess these skills can assess situations, identify obstacles and develop strategic plans to overcome them. Making sound decisions and solving problems pave the way for progress, enabling the organization to achieve its goals efficiently .

In today's dynamic business landscape, the ability to respond quickly and effectively to changes in the external environment is crucial. Leaders with strong decision-making and problem-solving skills can assess market trends, competitive forces and emerging opportunities, allowing them to make timely and informed decisions. This agility enables organizations to remain competitive, seize new opportunities and navigate uncertain times successfully.

Problem-solving and decision-making skills also are necessary for managing risk and minimizing consequences. Influential leaders possess the capacity to identify potential risks and evaluate different options for addressing them. They consider the possible implications of each decision and select the best course of action to minimize negative impacts. By carefully weighing risks and benefits, leaders can make informed decisions that mitigate potential pitfalls and maximize positive outcomes.

These skills also help to build trust and inspire loyalty. Making tough decisions and solving complex problems with confidence and clarity can significantly influence the dynamics within a team. When leaders exhibit competence in decision-making and problem-solving, team members gain trust in their abilities. This trust fosters a sense of security as team members believe their leader will make sound choices that benefit the organization and its members. In so doing, leaders inspire loyalty and commitment from their teams.

In essence, effective decision-making and problem-solving skills are foundational for leadership excellence. Leaders with these skills can navigate challenges, seize opportunities and guide their organizations to success. Their ability to adapt to changing circumstances, manage risks and inspire trust sets them apart, empowering them to make informed decisions that drive organizational growth and foster a positive team environment.

IMPROVE YOUR DECISION-MAKING AND PROBLEM-SOLVING SKILLS

Leaders can use different decision-making and problem-solving frameworks to make better choices. They provide structured approaches and guidelines that help leaders consider relevant factors, weigh alternatives and make informed decisions. Using these frameworks, they can systematically evaluate options, assess potential risks and rewards and consider different perspectives. The frameworks clarify complex decision-making situations, ensuring that leaders consider both logical reasoning and intuitive insights. They help influential leaders make better choices, increase the likelihood of positive outcomes and minimize the impact of biases or impulsive judgments. Some common decision-making frameworks include:

- **SWOT Analysis**

SWOT (strengths, weaknesses, opportunities and threats) analysis is a valuable framework to evaluate a company's competitive position and develop strategic planning. It enables a realistic, fact-based, data-driven assessment of an organization's strengths and weaknesses as well as those within its industry. To ensure accuracy, avoid preconceived beliefs or gray areas and focus on real-life contexts.

Think of the SWOT analysis as a guide rather than a rigid prescription. It uses internal and external data to guide businesses toward strategies that are more likely to succeed while steering them away from less successful approaches. Independent SWOT analysts, investors or competitors can also provide valuable insights into the strength or weakness of a company, product line or industry and the reasons behind it.

A comprehensive SWOT analysis encompasses four categories: strengths, weaknesses, opportunities and threats. Although the elements and findings within these categories vary across companies and situations, each component is essential for a thorough analysis.

"Strengths" highlight areas where an organization excels, differentiating it from the competition. This could include a strong brand, a loyal customer base, a robust balance sheet or unique technology. Conversely, "weaknesses" hinder optimal performance and require improvement to remain competitive. These might include a weak brand, high turnover rates, excessive debt, an inadequate supply chain or limited capital.

"Opportunities" refer to favorable external factors that can provide a competitive advantage to an organization. For example, reducing tariffs can enable a car manufacturer to enter a new market and increase sales and market share. On the other hand, "threats" encompass factors that can harm an organization, such as drought impacting a wheat-producing company's crop yield, rising material costs, intensifying competition or a shortage of skilled labor.

A SWOT analysis is broken down into several steps with actionable items before and after analyzing the four components. The process starts with determining a clear objective, as a focused analysis generates greater value. Once you have an objective, gather the necessary resources, including data and diverse perspectives. Compile ideas within each category, drawing from both internal and external factors. To refine your findings, prioritize and narrow down the ideas. It sets the stage for developing a strategy based on the ranked strengths, weaknesses, opportunities and threats.

- **Six Thinking Hats**

The Six Thinking Hats technique offers a structured approach to enhance idea-sharing and improvement by eliminating destructive elements during brainstorming meetings. It recognizes that human thinking can be unstructured and biased, hindering the objective of the design-thinking process. The method promotes sequential thinking and organized discussions by introducing six metaphorical hats representing different thinking types. While the technique deviates from ordinary thinking patterns, it can be effectively applied in critical thinking sessions to achieve specific targets such as problem-solving, argument discussions, in-depth analysis, planning processes and creative thinking.

The Six Hats method, originally developed to improve company investment returns, can be successfully adapted to various decision-making situations. The six hats include:

- **White Hat**

This hat focuses on sharing facts and information about the problem or argument. Stakeholders gather and present available information without engaging in further idea development. Questions in this phase revolve around available facts and information.

- **Yellow Hat**

The yellow hat encourages an optimistic perspective. Stakeholders consider the advantages and benefits of a proposed solution, shedding light on its positive aspects. Questions in this phase explore the solution's advantages and why it's deemed workable.

- **Black Hat**

Wearing the black hat prompts attendees to think cautiously and defensively. This phase aims to identify potential drawbacks and disadvantages of the proposal, analyzing its logical feasibility. Questions focus on risks, challenges and why the suggestion may not work.

- **Red Hat**

The red hat represents emotions and gut reactions. Stakeholders express their feelings about the problem or suggestion without delving into the reasoning behind them. Questions aim to understand emotional responses and gut reactions.

- **Green Hat**

The green hat symbolizes creative thinking. During this phase, stakeholders engage in innovative and creative thinking to find solutions to problems or explore suggestions from a fresh perspective.

- **Blue Hat**

The blue hat serves as the process control plan managed by meeting leaders. It ensures adherence to the technique's guidelines and directs the thinking process towards more productive routes. Facilitators may guide discussions to the green hat phase if ideas are lacking.

The hats' sequence and use during evaluation sessions may vary depending on the project, team and session's objectives. Use this framework if you want organized feedback from different perspectives, structured discussions and more effective decision-making.

- **Decision tree**

A decision tree visually represents interconnected choices and their potential outcomes. It enables individuals, teams or organizations to evaluate different actions by considering costs, probabilities and benefits. Decision trees facilitate informal discussions or construct algorithms for determining the optimal choice mathematically. Typically, it starts with a single node branching into various possible outcomes. Each outcome leads to additional nodes to create a tree-like structure.

There are three types of nodes in a decision tree: chance, decision and end nodes. A chance node, depicted as a circle, indicates the probabilities associated with specific results. A decision node, represented by a square, represents a decision that needs to be made. An end node, distinguished by a triangle, signifies the outcome of a decision path. To create a decision tree, select a medium, such as paper, a whiteboard or decision tree software. Follow these steps:

1. Start with the primary decision. Draw a small box to represent this point and a line extending to the right for each possible solution or action. Label accordingly.
2. Expand the tree by adding chance and decision nodes. If another decision is required, draw another box. If the outcome is uncertain, draw a circle (chance node). If the problem is resolved, leave it blank.
3. From each decision node, draw lines representing possible solutions. From each chance node, draw lines depicting potential outcomes. If you plan to analyze options quantitatively, include the probability and cost associated with each outcome and action.
4. Continue expanding the decision tree until every line reaches an end node, indicating that no further choices or chance outcomes need to be considered. Assign a value to each possible outcome, which could be a score or a financial value.

Decision trees are popular tools because they are easy to understand, can be used without concrete data and don't require much preparation. They are also flexible enough so that you can add new options when they come up and integrate them with other tools for decision-making. However, decision trees can become overly complex if not structured correctly.

Problem-Solving Frameworks

All the available problem-solving frameworks share a few things — they allow you to identify and understand the problem, facilitating brainstorming. However, some are better than others because they go a step further to connect the problem with your values and help you develop a way forward. The following frameworks are especially good at helping you do that:

- **IDEAL**

John Bransford and Barry Stein's problem-solving method, published in 1984 as a culmination of their research, is widely recognized and used in industry and education. It serves as a valuable tool to effectively identify problems, generate solutions and make progress. The IDEAL problem-solving method comprises the following steps:

- **I (Identify the Problem)** — To develop a solution, it is essential to understand the problem's scope. Articulate the problem in your own words, outlining the facts and unknowns.
- **D (Define an Outcome)** — The second step is establishing a clear outcome or goal. While multiple people may agree on the existence of a problem, they may have different ideas about the desired results. Defining a specific objective upfront can expedite the identification of solutions. The results and goals don't need to be complex; they should be clear to all parties involved.
- **E (Explore Possible Strategies)** — Brainstorm various strategies once an outcome is defined. During this stage, all potential solutions are considered. Make lists, use sticky notes or record ideas through voice memos. If you struggle with generating creative ideas, develop a plan and identify resources for further exploration.
- **A (Anticipate Outcomes & Act)** — After generating a list of strategies, the next IDEAL stage involves reviewing the potential steps and determining the best

initial course of action. Evaluating the pros and cons of each step. Pose questions like "What could happen if you take this step?" or "Do you feel confident or uncertain about this step?" After assessing the outcomes, take action, even if you are uncertain about the total result.

- **L (Look and Learn)** — This final step emphasizes reflecting on the attempt to solve the problem. It enables you to gain insights from both successful and unsuccessful problem-solving experiences. Ask questions such as "How did that go?" and "What changes would you make next time?"

By following the IDEAL problem-solving method and integrating the look-and-learn step, you can enhance the efficiency and effectiveness of your problem-solving skills.

- **Fishbone diagram**

A fishbone diagram is valuable for identifying numerous potential causes of an effect or problem. It provides a structured approach to brainstorming by categorizing ideas efficiently. This technique is beneficial when exploring possible causes for a problem or when thinking becomes stagnant. To utilize the fishbone diagram effectively, follow these steps:

1. **Make your team** — Bring together people who can provide insights and expertise relevant to the problem at hand.
2. **Define the problem** — Focus the session on the problem by clearly identifying the problem statement. Framing it as a "why" question can help generate answers and insights.

3. **Identify main categories** — Start considering the primary categories associated with the problem. This could include staff, software, marketing, budget, equipment, legal or other components. Write these labels in large category boxes at the top of the fishbone diagram.

4. **Find contributing causes** — Along the "fish bones," record all the contributing causes of the main problem under their respective categories.

5. **Name the root causes** — Continue identifying all the root causes underlying the various problems. Analyze the diagram with your team and determine how to address these issues effectively.

- **DMAIC**

The DMAIC (Defining, Measuring, Analyzing, Improving and Controlling) model is widely used to enhance the quality of outcomes produced by a company's processes. This data-driven cycle aims to optimize and stabilize business processes and designs. The DMAIC model consists of five phases, each serving a specific purpose:

1. Define.

Critical and impactful improvement opportunities are selected during this phase. The process is mapped and the problem's scope, focus and ultimate goal are established. Identify improvement opportunities, outline project scope and create a value stream map.

2. Measure.

This phase involves establishing baselines to assess the processes. You need sound benchmarks to track improvements. This phase includes developing data collection methods, recognizing input, processes and output indicators, collecting and analyzing current state data, outlining failure modes and effects analysis and implementing process capability analysis.

3. Analyze.

Here, you identify the underlying causes of problems and test them to facilitate improvement from the root level. Steps include conducting a complete root cause analysis, performing failure mode and effects analysis, using charts for visual representation of process variations, implementing process control and developing an improvement plan.

4. Improve.

Once the analysis is complete and data is available, focus on making actual improvements. Brainstorm and propose solution ideas, design experiments to determine expected benefits, revise process maps and plans based on previous data and outline test solutions and plans. Improvement management software can help streamline the process and ensure effective cross-functional collaboration.

5. Control.

This final phase ensures the long-term effectiveness and stability of implemented changes. It includes identifying and documenting the new work standards, developing a quality control plan, confirming failure reductions and monitoring execution. The control phase continues until new improvement opportunities arise and the DMAIC cycle restarts.

The structured nature of DMAIC allows you to track what works, eliminate ineffective process changes and continuously improve problem-solving approaches. The data collected throughout the process can also provide accurate baselines for future projects and assessments.

Leaders need specific skills to make the best decisions and practice effective problem-solving. They must be able to analyze complex situations, gather relevant information and consider various perspectives before arriving at a well-informed decision. Leaders must foster a collaborative and inclusive environment that encourages creativity, critical thinking and open communication among team members. By leveraging their analytical skills, sound judgment and strategic thinking, leaders can navigate challenges, make informed decisions and drive positive outcomes for their organizations. But it's not enough to make the right call. Once you know the best way forward, how do you communicate it to your team, colleagues and stakeholders so they get behind you? How do you communicate with impact?

8

COMMUNICATE WITH IMPACT

W e're now more interconnected than at any other time in history, but even though we constantly engage with others, miscommunication is still a pervasive challenge. The political activist and critic was onto something about communication. George Bernard Shaw's observation sums up the essence of this chapter: "The single biggest problem in communication is the illusion that it has taken place." Here, we will delve into the intricacies of communication and determine if your communication style is getting in the way of your leadership. This chapter explores the neuroscience of communication, uncovering the brain regions involved in verbal and nonverbal exchanges. By understanding the science behind how we communicate, we can equip ourselves with powerful techniques to improve our communication skills. Whether you aspire to be an influential leader or simply desire to forge stronger connections with those around you, this chapter explores the essential strategies to communicate with impact.

THE NEUROSCIENCE OF COMMUNICATION

Communication is often simplified as the transfer of information between individuals or groups. It involves a sender, a message and a recipient, forming the basic framework of any communication process. However, beneath this seemingly straightforward concept lies a rich tapestry of complexities. Message transmission is influenced by many factors, such as emotion, cultural context, communication medium and even physical surroundings. This intricacy renders good communication skills highly sought after by employers worldwide. Achieving accurate, effective and unambiguous communication is no easy feat.

Beyond the mere exchange of information, communication necessitates successful transmission and understanding of a message, whether it be information, ideas or emotions. The modes of communication are diverse with multiple forms often co-existing simultaneously. Verbal communication encompasses face-to-face interactions, telephone conversations, radio and television broadcasts, and other media. Nonverbal communication, on the other hand, extends to body language, gestures, attire, physical proximity and even olfactory signals. These subtle cues can convey messages unintentionally, making them significant components of your expressive repertoire. For instance, a change in tone of voice can reveal your mood, while hand signals and gestures can enhance verbal messages.

Nonverbal communication goes beyond words, utilizing facial expressions, hand gestures, eye contact (or lack thereof) and personal space among other nonverbal cues, to convey information. While some signals may operate subconsciously, research has identified nine distinct types of nonverbal communication. These include facial expressions, gestures, paralinguistics (such as vocal tone and loudness), body language, proxemics (personal space), eye gaze, haptics (touch), appearance and artifacts (objects and images).

In addition to verbal and nonverbal means, written communication plays a pivotal role in our modern world. Letters, emails, social media posts, books, magazines and online platforms have revolutionized the dissemination of written information. In the past, a select group of writers and publishers held significant power over written communication. Today, however, the digital age has democratized this domain, allowing anyone to express and publish their ideas online. This transformation has led to an explosion of information, disinformation and countless new avenues for communication.

As we explore the multifaceted nature of communication, it becomes clear that it's far more than a simple transmission of information. The process involves intricate dynamics influenced by various factors and encompasses various modes. Communication has nuances, and it pays to equip ourselves with the tools to become effective and impactful communicators. In every communication process, the ultimate objective is mutual understanding. However, disruptions at any stage can impede this goal. Let us consider the steps involved in the communication process:

First, a sender transmits a message through a communication channel to one or more receivers. The sender must encode the message, transforming it into a form suitable for the chosen medium. The receiver(s) then decode the message to grasp its meaning and significance.

Misunderstandings can arise at any point in the communication process, highlighting the need for effective communication to minimize confusion and overcome barriers. An adept communicator understands their audience, selects an appropriate communication channel, tailors their message to suit the medium and encodes it to reduce the likelihood of misunderstanding. They actively seek feedback from receivers to gauge their understanding and promptly address any misconceptions. Receivers can utilize techniques such as clarification and reflection to ensure an accurate interpretation of the message.

Communication channels are how we convey or receive messages. They play a vital role in transmitting information effectively. Today, we have numerous channels at our disposal. These include face-to-face conversations, phone calls, text messages, email, social media platforms like Facebook and Twitter, radio and TV broadcasts, written letters, brochures and reports. Choosing the appropriate communication channel is crucial for effective communication as each channel possesses distinct strengths and weaknesses.

For example, passing news about an upcoming event via a written letter may effectively reach a few individuals. Still, it may not be an efficient way to reach a large audience. On the other hand, conveying complex technical information is often more manageable through a printed document, allowing recipients to absorb the information at their own pace and revisit it as needed.

All messages must be encoded into a format suitable for the chosen communication channel. We encode messages daily when translating abstract thoughts into spoken or written words. However, different channels require distinct forms of encoding. For example, text written for a report may not be suitable for a radio program. The abbreviated language in text messages may be inappropriate for a letter or spoken conversation. Complex data may be best communicated through graphs, charts or other visualizations. Effective communicators know how to skillfully encode messages to match channels and intended audiences. They use appropriate language, convey information clearly and anticipate and address potential causes of confusion. They are mindful of recipients' past experiences in decoding similar communications.

Once received, the recipient must decode the message, which is also a vital communication skill. People interpret and understand messages differently, influenced by their experience, understanding of the message's context, familiarity with the sender, psychological state and the timing and environment of message reception. Additionally, communication barriers can impact decoding and understanding. Successful communicators anticipate and eliminate as many potential sources of misunderstanding as possible by understanding how the message will be decoded. They carefully consider recipients' perspectives and diligently work towards removing barriers.

Feedback forms the final part of the communication process, where the recipient informs the sender that they have received and understood the message. Recipients provide feedback through verbal and non-verbal reactions, allowing effective communicators to assess whether the message is understood as intended and rectify any confusion. It's important to note that the nature and extent of feedback varies depending on the communication channel. Face-to-face or phone conversations yield immediate and direct feedback. Feedback for messages conveyed through TV or radio may be indirect, delayed or even relayed through other channels such as the internet. Successful communicators value feedback as the primary means to evaluate comprehension and address any lingering confusion.

Communication involves a complex interplay of brain regions responsible for different aspects of speech, language and social interaction. Here are the parts of the brain that play the most significant roles:

- **Verbal communication**

Verbal communication refers to the use of words to pass a message. It includes both written and oral language, so as you interact with the following information, remember that it also includes written communication.

- **Broca's area**

Broca's area, named after French physician Paul Broca, is located in the frontal lobe, typically in the left hemisphere. It's associated specifically with speech production and language processing. The area's primary function is coordinating and executing complex motor movements required for producing articulate speech. It serves as the control center for the muscles involved in speech production, including the tongue, lips and vocal cords. Broca's area sends signals to the motor cortex when we speak , initiating a sequence of muscular movements necessary to make sounds and form words.

Damage to the area can result in a condition known as Broca's aphasia or expressive aphasia. Individuals with Broca's aphasia may struggle with producing fluent speech. Their speech tends to be slow, effortful and characterized by hesitations and difficulty finding words. Despite these difficulties, those with Broca's aphasia often maintain their understanding of language and are aware of the impairments in their speech.

Research has also revealed that Broca's area involves more than just speech production. It contributes to various aspects of language processing, including syntactic processing and grammatical comprehension. Studies show that Broca's area plays a role in sentence comprehension, grammatical rule generation and the processing of complex grammatical structures. It helps you interpret and understand language structure, allowing you to construct meaningful sentences and comprehend the intentions behind others' speech. It collaborates closely with other brain regions, such as Wernicke's area in the left temporal lobe, which is associated with language comprehension. The connection between Broca's area and Wernicke's area, known as the arcuate fasciculus, facilitates the exchange of information between these two regions, allowing for seamless communication between language production and comprehension processes.

- **Wernicke's area**

Wernicke's area is named after the German neurologist Carl Wernicke. It is a critical region of the brain associated with language comprehension and the processing of spoken and written language. It's located in the posterior part of the left superior temporal gyrus, typically in the dominant hemisphere (usually the left hemisphere for right-handed individuals). The primary function of Wernicke's area is language comprehension and interpretation. When you listen to someone speaking or read written words, Wernicke's area helps you understand the meaning of the words and construct coherent mental representations of language.

Damage to Wernicke's area can result in a condition known as Wernicke's aphasia or receptive aphasia. Individuals with Wernicke's aphasia may have difficulties comprehending spoken or written language, even though they produce speech fluently. Their speech may be articulate but often lacks meaningful content and may include nonsensical words. Importantly, individuals with Wernicke's aphasia are often unaware of their language comprehension deficits and may not recognize the errors they make in their speech.

- **Non-verbal communication**

A substantial portion of communication is non-verbal. Non-verbal communication is the process of conveying a message without using words. It's dependent on expressions and physical movement. The following parts of the brain are involved in non-verbal communication:

- **The superior temporal gyrus**

The superior temporal gyrus (STG) is a significant brain region involved in various cognitive processes, including nonverbal communication. Located in the temporal lobe, the STG encompasses several subregions contributing different aspects of nonverbal communication. A vital function of the STG in nonverbal communication is processing auditory information. The region is responsible for perceiving and interpreting various auditory cues, such as tone of voice, intonation and emotional prosody. It helps you discern the emotional and expressive qualities conveyed through someone's voice, allowing you to understand their feelings and intentions even without explicit verbal content.

The STG also plays a crucial role in processing facial expressions. It is involved in the perception and recognition of facial emotional expressions such as happiness, sadness, fear, anger and surprise. By connecting with other brain regions, including the amygdala and fusiform face area, the STG helps you interpret and respond to facial cues, enabling you to gauge the emotional states of others and adjust your own nonverbal behavior accordingly.

- **The insula**

The insula also plays a significant role in nonverbal communication. Although traditionally associated with processing internal bodily sensations, the insula is involved in various aspects of nonverbal communication, particularly emotional and empathetic responses. One crucial function is the processing of emotions. The insula helps you experience and recognize your own emotions as well as perceive and empathize with the feelings of others. By connecting with other brain regions involved in emotion processing, such as the amygdala and prefrontal cortex, the insula contributes to your ability to interpret and respond to emotional cues in facial expressions, body language and vocal intonations. It helps you discern subtle emotional nuances to understand and empathize with others' emotions accurately.

The insula is also involved in interoception, which is the perception and awareness of bodily sensations and internal physiological states. Interoception provides valuable information about your own physical and emotional states. This inner awareness can influence nonverbal communication as bodily sensations can manifest in your gestures, facial expressions and overall body language. The insula plays a role in integrating interoceptive signals and linking them to emotional and cognitive processes, contributing to the nonverbal expression and interpretation of your internal state.

- **The amygdala**

The amygdala plays a crucial role in processing emotional and social cues. As part of the limbic system, it's involved in forming, recognizing and regulating emotions, all key components of nonverbal communication. One of the amygdala's primary functions in nonverbal communication is recognizing and interpreting facial expressions. It helps you quickly and automatically identify emotional facial expressions such as fear, happiness, anger and sadness. Through its connections with visual processing regions, such as the fusiform face area, the amygdala facilitates the rapid assessment of emotional cues in faces, enabling you to gauge the emotional states of others and respond accordingly.

Additionally, the amygdala is involved in processing emotional significance and salience. It assigns emotional value and determines the relevance and importance of incoming sensory information, including nonverbal cues. This allows you to prioritize and attend to emotionally meaningful signals in your environment. The amygdala's role in assigning emotional salience helps shape your nonverbal communication by influencing your attention, perception and response to social and emotional cues.

It also plays a vital role in the experience and regulation of emotions during social interactions. It helps generate and modulate emotional responses, facilitating appropriate emotional reactions in different social contexts. The amygdala's involvement in emotional processing allows you to convey and understand emotions through nonverbal channels, such as facial expressions, vocal intonations and body language.

COMMUNICATION SKILLS IN LEADERSHIP

Effective communication plays a pivotal role in the success of leaders and organizations, encompassing various important aspects. It helps you articulate your vision, goals and expectations. When effectively conveying this information, you align everyone toward a common purpose. Research has found that team members can work harmoniously towards shared goals when they understand the overarching objectives and their individual roles and responsibilities.

Effective communication enables leaders to build strong relationships with their team members. Open and transparent communication fosters trust, promotes understanding and creates a positive work environment. When team members feel valued and understood, they are more engaged, motivated and willing to collaborate, leading to higher productivity and satisfaction.

Good communication skills are essential for leaders to address team conflicts, concerns and challenges. By fostering an open and non-judgmental communication environment, they encourage team members to voice their opinions, share their perspectives and resolve conflicts constructively. Effective communication helps leaders to listen actively, understand different viewpoints and find mutually beneficial solutions. It allows them to provide timely and constructive feedback to their team members, which can help individuals grow, improve their performance and develop their skills. Constructive feedback, when communicated effectively, motivates team members, boosts morale and contributes to a culture of continuous learning and development.

Leaders who possess strong communication skills are more likely to achieve their goals and objectives. Clear communication ensures team members are aligned and focused on the desired outcomes. It promotes effective planning, coordination and execution of tasks, maximizing the chances of achieving desired results. To communicate effectively, you need various skills that work harmoniously together. These skills encompass various aspects, including verbal expression, body language and emotional intelligence. They also include:

- **Listening skills**

Active listening is the foundation of clear communication. As an effective communicator, you prioritize listening over speaking, attentively absorbing what others contribute to the conversation. You employ different listening styles, paying close attention to the message and making others feel valued and understood.

- **Empathy**

Understanding the emotions of those around you is vital to effective communication. Empathy involves understanding and relating to the feelings of others. Demonstrating high emotional intelligence and the ability to empathize helps you build rapport, foster stronger connections and enhance your communication effectiveness.

- **Nonverbal communication skills**

Effective communication extends beyond verbal messages. Nonverbal cues, such as body language and tone of voice, play a significant role in conveying messages accurately. By developing an awareness of these nonverbal aspects, you boost your messaging and presentation skills as well as overall communication effectiveness.

- **Teamwork**

Engaging in teamwork and consistently collaborating with coworkers is crucial for building strong business communication skills. The stronger the connections, the more effectively you can communicate and collaborate with team members.

As it is, not all communication in the workplace is created equal. We've all been through those never-ending meetings that could have been condensed into a simple email. Different types of communication require different channels to convey the message effectively. A skilled communicator understands this and adapts their approach accordingly. At work, you will use other types of communication, including leadership communication. This tends to be one-way communication with your team. It happens when you need to inform or update employees about new policies or changes in direction. Additionally, leaders communicate to persuade, encourage and inspire commitment. In these instances, stories often carry more weight than raw data.

In upward communication, you may find yourself communicating with higher-level managers or leaders who aren't directly in your chain of command. This type of communication is usually more formal and includes memos, emails, reports or meeting presentations. It's essential to consider the format and convey information concisely and professionally. You may also be required to give updates. Updates are typically brief, so it's essential to use visual trackers or dashboards to convey the necessary information. Save your verbal or written commentary to draw attention to what requires action or further involvement. Highlight surprises, obstacles, potential risks and wins to ensure the audience focuses on the most critical aspects.

For presentations, the tone is formal. Presentations are aimed at a larger audience and carry higher stakes. Objectives may include informing, influencing and persuading. Thanks to platforms like TED, audiences now expect informative and entertaining presentations. At work, communication also happens in meetings. Meetings are often one of the most misunderstood and overused forms of communication. Effective meetings foster collaboration and quickly communicate information that might be misunderstood in other formats like email. The best sessions leave participants feeling energized rather than drained.

There are also customer communications in the workplace. When communicating with customers, the same considerations apply to internal communication. Interactions can range from one-off to face-to-face, virtual, spoken or written exchanges. It's crucial to be deliberate in planning messages to provide what the customer needs in a way they prefer. Customer communication should create a positive impression for the company and its products.

You'll also have informal interactions in the workplace, such as daily emails and chats to make requests, seek information and provide support. These interactions not only drive the organization forward but also serve secondary objectives. They help form social connections, build a positive company culture, establish trust and find common ground among colleagues.

Clearly, effective workplace communication requires understanding the different types of communication and adapting to the appropriate channels and approaches. There is a lot to gain from cultivating better communication skills at work. Good communication is like the secret sauce that can transform your team dynamics and drive success. When communication is strong, employees feel more engaged in their work. They understand their contributions are valued and make a difference. This sense of value and recognition fuels their motivation to give their best. Engaged employees become key contributors to the company's productivity and are more likely to stay with the organization.

As noted earlier, effective communication helps employees understand their roles and how their work contributes to the overall success of the team and organization. This clarity fosters a sense of pride and purpose, boosting job satisfaction and morale. Employees who feel connected to their work and understand its significance bring more energy and enthusiasm to their tasks. Additionally, effective communication reduces churn. It reduces turnover by playing a crucial role in employee satisfaction and engagement. When employees feel heard, valued and understood, they are likelier to stay with the company, contributing to its stability and success.

IMPROVE YOUR COMMUNICATION SKILLS

Effective communication is a critical skill for all leaders. It is also a learnable skill. If you want to work on improving how you communicate, there are places you can start:

Verbal Communication

- **Think about it.**

When it comes to communication, it's important to start by thinking through a few key questions. Ask yourself, "Why are you communicating? Who is the audience? What is your goal? What do you want the recipient to do?" And finally, "What format will best achieve your objective?" If you're having trouble answering these questions, take time to reflect on your communication approach and seek feedback from colleagues or your manager.

- **Do not rush it.**

Effective communication requires planning and review. Take time to plan what you want to say and ensure your message is achieving its intended purpose. This is especially true for written communication — revise, revise, revise! Remember, great communication may appear effortless but often requires careful thought and crafting.

- **Simplify it.**

In the workplace, people are busy, so ensure your message is easy to understand and act upon. Clearly state your objective and main point from the beginning, whether in a presentation or written communication. Then, provide the necessary details to support your main message. Don't make communication unnecessarily complicated, so find a clear and straightforward way to express your point. Repeat it throughout your communication and consider using visual aids or metaphors to make it memorable and easily understandable.

- **Try different approaches.**

To enhance your communication skills, try different approaches for different communication needs. Focus on one aspect at a time. For example, spend a week paying extra attention to structuring informal communications, then try different structures for formal meetings or updates. Experimentation will help you find what works best for different situations.

- **Practice and reflect.**

Actively reflect on your day-to-day communications and identify areas for improvement. If an email to your manager didn't go well, consider how it might be misinterpreted and what you could do differently next time. Similarly, if a conversation with a coworker didn't yield the expected results, assess whether you effectively communicate your needs.

- **Watch your tone.**

Your tone of voice carries much meaning and can significantly influence how others respond to you. Experiment with different tones to emphasize your ideas effectively. For instance, an animated tone of voice can convey genuine interest and generate interest in your listeners.

- **Request feedback.**

Don't be afraid to ask for feedback from trusted coworkers and your manager. Request separate ratings for your written and spoken communication skills. Additionally, ask them what's one thing you should start doing, stop doing or focus on to improve your communication in the organization. Constructive feedback is invaluable for personal growth.

As a rule of thumb, develop a filter. Effective communicators have finely tuned social skills, knowing what's appropriate to express in different contexts. Having a filter ensures you maintain professionalism, decorum and avoid unnecessary conflicts in the workplace.

Non-Verbal Communication

Communication goes beyond words. Here are some ways to pay attention to your nonverbal cues, learn how they contribute to your overall communication and work to improve them:

- **Watch for incongruence.**

Pay attention when someone's words don't align with their nonverbal behaviors. For instance, if someone says they are happy but their facial expression and body language suggest otherwise, it's important to take note of these inconsistencies. Incongruent behaviors can provide valuable insights into a person's thoughts and emotions.

- **Keep eye contact.**

Maintaining appropriate eye contact is crucial for effective nonverbal communication. It signals attentiveness and builds trust. However, striking the right balance is critical. For example, too little eye contact may seem elusive, while excessive eye contact can be seen as aggressive. Aim for natural and comfortable eye contact, typically lasting three to four seconds.

- **Do not be afraid to ask.**

If you feel confused by someone's nonverbal signals, don't hesitate to ask questions for clarification. Reciting your interpretation of what was said and seeking further explanation can help present or resolve misunderstandings and encourage open communication. Active listening and demonstrating genuine interest through questions can enhance the conversation.

- **Use gestures and signals to add meaning.**

Verbal and nonverbal communication work together to convey messages effectively. You enhance your spoken communication by aligning your body language with your words. For example, maintaining a self-assured stance with a firm posture and balanced body weight can help convey confidence during presentations. Facial expressions, gestures and personal space also play significant roles in nonverbal communication.

- **Consider signals as a whole.**

It's important to consider the full context rather than focusing on isolated signals to accurately interpret nonverbal behavior. A single gesture or expression may not provide the complete picture. Look for groups of signals that reinforce a common message. By taking a holistic approach, you can avoid misinterpreting nonverbal communication. Always consider the situation and context in which communication takes place. Different settings may require varying levels of formality and appropriate nonverbal behaviors. Adjust your nonverbal signals to ensure they align with the situation and effectively convey your intended message.

Remember that nonverbal signals can be misinterpreted or influenced by various factors, so avoid making assumptions based on a single gesture or behavior. Instead, observe a person's overall demeanor and consider what factors may impact their nonverbal communication. Developing interpersonal skills and emotional intelligence can help you accurately interpret nonverbal signals. Of course, this will take practice. Improving nonverbal communication is not a skill you develop overnight. Pay close attention to nonverbal behaviors, both in yourself and in others. Experiment with different types of nonverbal communication in various interactions and give yourself time to practice them.

Notably, communication is complex and multifaceted. There is no one-size-fits-all approach. However, you can become a more effective communicator by increasing your awareness of nonverbal signals, their impact on interpersonal relationships and how you use your verbal skills. You can become the kind of leader whose words move and inspire. And who doesn't want that? In the next chapter, we will explore the interplay between leadership and productivity, so that when you inspire your team to be busy, they're busy with the right things.

9

MAXIMIZE PRODUCTIVITY

In a world where demands on our time seem endless, it has become increasingly important not just to be busy, but to be productive. But how can we, as leaders, truly make the most of our time and accomplish our goals efficiently? This chapter discusses the neuroscience of time and explores the intricate connection between time management, productivity and the workings of our brain. Drawing inspiration from author Henry David Thoreau's timeless words, this chapter seeks to go beyond mere busyness and instead focuses on the true essence of productivity. By understanding the neuroscience behind effective time management and productivity, you can unlock the secrets to optimizing your cognitive abilities and achieving greater success in your personal and professional lives.

HOW THE BRAIN PROCESSES TIME AND ENHANCES PRODUCTIVITY

Do you ever feel like you could use more hours in your day? No matter how hard we try, there's always something left undone or a task we can't seem to get to. So why do some people seem to achieve more with their time than others? The answer lies in good time management. Time management is organizing and planning how to divide your time between different activities. It's about working smarter, not harder, to accomplish more in less time, even when the pressures are high and time is tight. The highest achievers understand the importance of managing their time exceptionally well.

Effective time management encompasses several vital elements. First, there's effective planning. Planning your day and creating a task plan or to-do list can make a significant difference. Write down the essential activities that need to be done and allocate the appropriate amount of time to each task. Start with high-priority work and move on to tasks that require less immediate attention. Complete one before moving on to the next and mark off completed tasks as you go to track your progress.

Setting goals and objectives is another crucial aspect of time management. Without clear targets, it's easy to lose your way. Set realistic and achievable goals in your personal and professional lives. These goals act as guiding stars, giving you direction and purpose. Time management also involves setting deadlines. Deadlines keep you on track and prevent procrastination. Don't wait for others to set deadlines for you — take ownership of your work and establish realistic timeframes for each task. Use a planner, calendar or app to mark important dates and deadlines, helping you stay organized and focused.

The fourth component of time management is the delegation of responsibilities. Good time management demands that you learn to say "no" when necessary and not try to do everything on your own. It calls you to recognize other people can contribute their skills and expertise. Delegate tasks based on employees' interests and specialization so tasks are completed within deadlines. Remember that different individuals require different amounts of time to accomplish the same task, so delegate accordingly.

Finally, good time management requires prioritization and spending the right amount of time on the right activity. It requires you to identify the importance and urgency of each task and allocate your time accordingly. Learn to differentiate between what's truly important and what can wait. Tackle tasks with the highest priority first to ensure they receive the necessary attention and focus. Alongside this, commit to spending the right amount of time on the right activity. The best leaders have learned to do the right thing at the right time. They won't waste an entire day on a task that could be finished in an hour.

When you hone your time management skills, you unlock numerous benefits. You become more productive and efficient, reducing stress and increasing your confidence. Managing your time well helps build a better professional reputation, opens up opportunities for advancement and increases your chances of achieving your goals. Good time management will give you more control of your time, allowing you to assist others in reaching their targets as well. It's a win-win situation.

So, take a moment to reflect on your time management habits. What causes stress and hinders your ability to manage your time effectively? Consider the benefits you'll gain when practicing effective time management:

- A better work-life balance
- Increased time freedom
- Higher levels of productivity
- Less procrastination
- Simplicity
- Reduced distractions
- Increased energy

- More time to think and plan

Visualize how these improvements would transform your life and create a clear action plan to make them a reality. Remember, time is a limited resource, but how you manage it is within your control.

Researchers have proposed three key elements, often called the "3 Ps," of effective time management. They are planning, prioritizing and performing. As the saying goes, "By failing to plan, you are planning to fail." Without proper planning, you may be unprepared, facing unexpected challenges, missing deadlines and risking your reputation. Planning allows you to clearly understand what needs to be done to ensure the success of a project or task. It helps you stay organized, reduce stress and avoid feeling overwhelmed.

After creating a comprehensive task list and allocating time during planning, the next step is to prioritize. Prioritizing helps you determine which tasks will bring the most value and impact. It involves identifying the most important task and then ranking the others accordingly. It's helpful to categorize tasks into different groups based on their urgency and importance. Most of your time and effort should go to tasks under the "important and not urgent" category. These are tasks that require action and have long-term significance.

The final P stands for performing. Once you have planned and prioritized your tasks, it's crucial to focus on one task at a time and complete it without distractions. Your performance demands concentration without distraction. It requires you to pay attention to your energy levels and perform essential tasks when most alert and energetic.

Time management and productivity are closely linked to the brain's executive function, which includes planning, organization and decision-making. Expectedly, different parts of the brain play a role in productivity, including:

- **The prefrontal cortex**

This region at the front of the brain is responsible for executive functions, including planning, decision-making, goal-setting and self-control. These cognitive processes are essential for effective time management and optimal productivity. The prefrontal cortex plays a significant role in the ability to plan and organize. It helps you create a roadmap for tasks and activities, allowing you to allocate time and resources appropriately. The prefrontal cortex enables you to break down complex tasks into manageable steps, set realistic deadlines and create schedules or to-do lists. By engaging this region, you can outline the necessary actions and establish a clear plan to achieve your goals.

The prefrontal cortex also contributes to your ability to prioritize tasks. It helps you evaluate the importance and urgency of different activities and make decisions based on their significance. This region assists in determining which tasks require immediate attention and that can be deferred. By activating the prefrontal cortex, you can allocate your time and energy to the most important and impactful activities, maximizing productivity.

Finally, the prefrontal cortex plays a vital role in self-regulation and self-control. It helps you resist distractions, stay focused on your goals and manage impulses that may hinder productivity. This region helps override immediate gratification and maintain a long-term perspective. Activating the prefrontal cortex helps you resist the temptation to engage in unproductive activities and stay committed to your tasks.

- **The basal ganglia**

While the basal ganglia are primarily associated with motor control, they also play a significant role in habit formation and reinforcement learning. Regarding motor control, the basal ganglia act as a central hub that integrates information from various parts of the brain, including the cortex and thalamus, to facilitate the initiation, modulation and execution of voluntary movements. They help refine motor actions by regulating the motor cortex's activity and controlling the motor pathways' output.

The basal ganglia have several vital structures, including the striatum, globus pallidus, substantia nigra and subthalamic nucleus. The striatum, the basal ganglia's central input region, receives information from the cortex and other brain regions. It is a gatekeeper, filtering and selecting relevant information to guide motor actions.

The basal ganglia also play a crucial role in habit formation. Habits are automatic and repetitive behaviors performed with little conscious effort. The basal ganglia, and other brain regions like the prefrontal cortex and hippocampus, are involved in forming and executing habits. Through a process known as reinforcement learning, the basal ganglia help in shaping and strengthening habits based on rewards and punishments. When you engage in rewarded behavior, the basal ganglia reinforce the neural connections associated with that behavior, making it more likely to be repeated. Over time, through repeated reinforcement, the behavior becomes automatic and ingrained as a habit.

- **The dopamine system**

The basal ganglia's involvement in habit formation is closely tied to the dopamine system. The brain's reward system, specifically the release of dopamine, plays a crucial role in productivity. Dopamine is a neurotransmitter associated with pleasure, motivation and reward. When you accomplish tasks or achieve goals, the brain's reward system releases dopamine. This surge of dopamine reinforces your behavior and motivates you to continue engaging in productive activities.

On the other hand, procrastination is attributed to a lack of dopamine release in response to tasks. When you perceive a task as uninteresting, overwhelming or lacking immediate rewards, the brain's reward system doesn't activate as strongly. As a result, you may experience a lack of motivation, feelings of overwhelm and a tendency to avoid or delay the task. Procrastination becomes a habitual response when the brain fails to associate completing the task with a rewarding dopamine release.

It's important to note that multitasking is not an effective strategy for productivity. While some individuals may believe they are proficient multitaskers, research shows that human brains aren't designed to handle multiple tasks simultaneously. When we attempt to multitask, we switch our attention rapidly between tasks, which incurs a cognitive cost known as "switching cost." This switching cost leads to reduced efficiency, decreased focus and increased errors.

Multitasking taxes the brain's cognitive resources by requiring you to constantly shift your attention, allocate mental resources to different tasks and readjust your focus. As a result, the quality of your work may suffer, taking longer to complete tasks compared to focusing on them one at a time. Instead of multitasking, it's more effective to prioritize tasks, allocate dedicated time blocks to focus on each task and give your full attention to one task at a time.

TIME MANAGEMENT AND PRODUCTIVITY IN LEADERSHIP

Effective time management and productivity are essential aspects of leadership that directly impact the success and effectiveness of leaders in various fields. Leaders who effectively manage their time and enhance productivity can accomplish more in less time. By prioritizing tasks, setting goals and allocating resources efficiently, they can optimize their work processes and achieve better results. This enables leaders to make the most of their available time and drive progress in their organizations.

Leaders who demonstrate effective time management and productivity set a positive example for their team members. When they value and respect time, it encourages subordinates to do the same. This fosters a culture of efficiency and productivity within the organization, ultimately leading to higher performance and success.

Additionally, time management plays a crucial role in meeting deadlines and achieving goals. Leaders who effectively manage their time are better equipped to plan and organize their activities, ensuring tasks are done on schedule. Because they meet deadlines consistently, these leaders build trust, enhance credibility and instill a sense of accountability within their teams.

Effective time management enables leaders to allocate sufficient time for critical decision-making processes. When they clearly understand priorities and deadlines, they can allow time for analysis, reflection and consultation. This allows for thoughtful and well-informed decision-making, leading to more successful outcomes and minimizing the chances of hasty or ill-informed choices. These leaders are more productive. Productivity in leadership involves making the most of available resources, including time. Effective time management ensures leaders utilize their time to align with their strategic objectives.

Poor time management often leads to increased stress levels for leaders. Efficient time management helps reduce stress and prevent burnout. Proper time allocation allows for adequate breaks, self-care and work-life balance. A leader who maintains a healthy balance is better equipped to handle challenges, make sound decisions and lead effectively. They can adapt and be agile in a dynamic environment. These leaders set aside time for planning, reflection and learning, which keeps them updated with industry trends, helps them anticipate changes and adjust their strategies accordingly. This agility helps them promptly respond to emerging opportunities and challenges, giving their organizations a competitive edge.

Leaders with strong time management and prioritization skills can plan priorities. They understand the importance of setting clear objectives and goals for themselves and their teams. These leaders invest time in thoughtful planning, analyzing tasks and identifying the most critical and impactful priorities. By planning, they ensure their efforts align with the organization's strategic objectives and that they can guide their team to success.

The icing on the cake is that strong time management skills help leaders balance the tension between daily tasks and strategic action. They recognize the importance of not getting caught up solely in the day-to-day operations but also dedicating time to strategic thinking and long-term planning. They understand that while daily tasks require attention, allocating time for strategic actions is crucial for sustained growth and success. By finding the right balance, leaders navigate the present while keeping an eye on the future.

Essentially, leaders with solid time management and prioritization skills excel in allocating time effectively across multiple priorities. They understand time is a finite resource and make conscious decisions about using it. These leaders assess each task's importance, urgency and impact and prioritize accordingly. They are skilled at managing competing demands and allocating appropriate time to address all essential activities.

They know how to set time boundaries and build healthy habits. They understand the importance of establishing limitations to protect their time and avoid unnecessary distractions. They create a focused work environment with efficient time utilization by setting clear expectations around their availability, delegating tasks and managing interruptions. Additionally, these leaders prioritize self-care and establish healthy habits such as regular breaks, exercise and adequate rest. They recognize that maintaining their well-being is essential for sustained productivity and optimal performance.

IMPROVE TIME MANAGEMENT AND PRODUCTIVITY

It is clear so far that you have so much to gain from better time management. Effective time management will help you hit your goals by allowing you to allocate enough time each day to work on them and be productive. The following tips will make that possible for you:

- **Priorities over emergencies.**

As a leader, it's all too common to become entangled in the never-ending cycle of resolving emergencies. However, to truly excel, you have to shift focus onto your priorities. Take a moment to deeply reflect upon your priorities — for yourself, your team, your company and beyond. More often than not, emergencies don't align with your core priorities. While they may demand attention and awareness, they frequently serve as distractions that can divert you from your intended path. Recognize that you may not need to personally address every emergency, even if you do need to be informed about them.

Once you've gained clarity on your priorities, brace yourself to firmly decline engagements that don't align with them. Learn the power of explicitly saying "no" to anything that detracts from your focus. Doing so creates boundaries that preserve your time and energy for things that genuinely matter and contribute to your desired outcomes. When you encounter a task at work that you are unsure where it falls — whether it's a priority or a task — there are strategies you can use for prioritization, including:

- **Consolidate your tasks into one list.**

Achieving effective prioritization starts with fully understanding all the tasks at hand. Even seemingly mundane or routine activities should be acknowledged and recorded. To gain a holistic view, merge personal and work-related tasks into a single, centralized task list. From scheduling important meetings with superiors to mundane errands like picking up dry cleaning, capturing everything in one place ensures no task is overlooked. Once all tasks are documented, prioritization can occur based on factors such as importance, urgency, duration and potential rewards.

- **Identify and align with overarching goals.**

Prioritization is not just a short-term time management strategy; it plays a pivotal role in accomplishing long-term goals. Understanding the ultimate objectives you are working towards, whether a promotion, project completion or a career transition, helps identify tasks directly contributing to those desired outcomes. It's helpful to break down large goals into smaller, time-specific milestones. By deconstructing yearly goals into monthly to-do lists, which further translate into weekly tasks and daily priorities, you can focus and ensure alignment with your long-term goals.

- **Highlight the urgent.**

An effective to-do list should provide a clear overview of impending deadlines, enabling you to identify tasks that require immediate attention and plan. Establish self-imposed deadlines, even for non-time-sensitive tasks, to prevent essential responsibilities from being continually postponed. This enhances productivity, reduces procrastination and facilitates better planning and use of available time.

- **Prioritize based on importance and urgency.**

In his book, "The 7 Habits of Highly Effective People," renowned businessman Stephen Covey suggests categorizing and prioritizing tasks based on importance and urgency. Tasks falling under "urgent and important" categories should be addressed first. For "important but not urgent" tasks, allocate dedicated time on your calendar to ensure uninterrupted focus on their completion. Delegate tasks that are "urgent but unimportant." It will empower your team members and free up your own time.

- **Mitigate competing priorities.**

Managing multiple tasks simultaneously becomes increasingly challenging as their complexity grows. Research indicates that people in positions of power tend to prioritize a single goal, while those in lower-ranking positions continue to juggle multiple competing priorities. However, attempting to handle concurrent tasks leads to a decline in performance, compromising the quality of the most important tasks. To stay focused on crucial responsibilities, identify likely distractions, such as concurrent tasks or ad-hoc requests, and actively avoid them.

- **Consider the effort required.**

When confronted with an extensive to-do list, it's easy to feel overwhelmed, leading to decreased productivity and potential procrastination. A valuable strategy to overcome this hurdle involves assessing tasks based on the effort required to complete them. If the list becomes burdensome, prioritizing tasks requiring minimal time and effort allows for quick completion and generates a sense of accomplishment. Promptly clearing these tasks creates breathing space and instills motivation to tackle the remaining workload throughout the day.

- **Constantly review your progress.**

Productivity consultant David Allen, the proponent of the "Get Things Done" (GTD) methodology, emphasizes the importance of critical reflection. Regularly reviewing task lists and priorities is crucial for regaining control and focus. Constant assessment allows for adjustments based on changing circumstances, ensuring that tasks and priorities remain aligned with objectives. Be realistic about expectations and timelines; it will make you more productive.

- **Organize yourself.**

To help maximize efficiency, establish personalized systems and structures that facilitate task management. Whether you prefer a digital task list, a synchronized calendar, a physical whiteboard or even a unique 3D model, find a method that suits your working style and supports tracking commitments and deadlines. Your chosen system must allow you to carve out uninterrupted time dedicated solely to your priorities, safeguarding them from being infringed upon by meetings or distractions. Schedule dedicated time for leadership responsibilities, progress on individual projects and mentorship of emerging leaders.

- **Delegate strategically instead of getting sidetracked.**

One common pitfall among leaders is the tendency to shoulder excessive responsibility. Instead of trying to do everything yourself, effective leadership entails delegating tasks to capable team members. Delegation frees up your time, empowers your team and fosters their professional growth. When assigning tasks, be clear about your expectations, providing specific instructions and deadlines. Allow your team members the space to learn and develop, offering constructive feedback to guide their future contributions.

- **Cultivate a culture of accountability.**

Accountability ensures you meet goals and appropriately manage priorities Start by setting clear expectations and communicating them to your team members. Clearly outline goals and deadlines and hold individuals accountable for meeting them. Provide regular feedback to support their growth and lead by example. If you expect your team members to be accountable, you must exemplify accountability yourself, being responsible for your commitments and each team member.

Being a leader doesn't mean having all the answers or handling every task independently. The most efficient environments thrive on collaboration and seeking assistance when needed. Authentic leadership involves embracing humility, recognizing when to seek help and demonstrating unwavering commitment and consistency in pursuing your priorities. You create an environment conducive to productivity, growth and successful outcomes by nurturing these qualities.

- **Use time-blocking to schedule your days.**

Time-blocking is an effective time management method that involves dividing your day into dedicated blocks of time for specific tasks. Instead of relying on a flexible to-do list that allows you to tackle tasks whenever you find time, time-blocking requires creating a structured schedule at the beginning of each day. The key to this method is prioritizing your tasks in advance, necessitating a regular weekly review. By assessing upcoming commitments and responsibilities for the week ahead, you can sketch a rough plan for time blocks each day. At the end of each workday, take a moment to review unfinished tasks and any new ones that have emerged, adjusting your time blocks for the rest of the week accordingly.

With a predetermined time-blocked schedule, you no longer need to constantly decide what to focus on. All you have to do is follow your plan, refer to it whenever you get off-task or distracted and swiftly return to the designated task for that time block. Time-blocking has several related approaches that offer similar benefits, including:

- **Task-batching**

Task-batching involves grouping similar tasks and allocating specific time blocks to complete them simultaneously. Focusing on similar tasks consecutively minimizes context switching during your day, saving time and mental energy. For example, dedicating two 20-minute time blocks to process email is more efficient than checking your inbox every 15 minutes. Time-blocking pairs well with task-batching, eliminating the need to schedule individual tasks on your calendar. Instead, block off chunks of time each day or week to complete specific groups of activities, such as email, invoicing, workouts, meetings, writing, coding, deep work or errands.

- **Day-theming**

Day-theming takes task-batching to a more extreme level and is particularly useful for people with multiple areas of responsibility vying for their attention. Rather than assigning time blocks for each area of responsibility daily, day-theming designates an entire day each week for each distinct duty. This approach creates a reliable work pattern and reduces the cognitive load associated with frequent context switching. For example, an entrepreneur may dedicate one day to marketing, another to sales, etc. This allows for focused attention and mental clarity, ensuring optimal productivity in each area.

- **Time-boxing**

Time-boxing, often mistaken as synonymous with time-blocking, has a distinct difference. While time-blocking involves setting aside specific chunks of time to concentrate on a particular task or activity (e.g., working on a blog post from 9-11 a.m.), time-boxing imposes a limit on how much time you allocate for a specific task (e.g., finishing a first draft of a blog post between 9-11 a.m.). This self-imposed "time box" encourages efficient work by creating a sense of urgency within a predetermined time frame. It can be an enjoyable way to challenge yourself, adding an element of gamification to your productivity efforts.

A key advantage of time-blocking is its ability to promote focused "deep work." Dedicating uninterrupted chunks of time to a single project or task brings your full mental resources and concentration to bear on that particular activity. Cal Newport, author of "Deep Work: Rules for Focused Success in a Distracted World," highlights the productivity generated by time-blocking. He suggests that a structured 40-hour time-blocked workweek can produce the same output as a 60+ hour workweek without structure. Engaging in deep work consistently through time-blocking strengthens the mental muscles required for sustained focus and increases productivity.

Additionally, time-blocking facilitates the efficient completion of "shallow work," which refers to urgent tasks not important for long-term goals. Setting clear limits on time allocated to shallow work and grouping similar tasks minimizes costs associated with context switching. You power through these tasks more efficiently, freeing up the rest of the workday for higher-impact and more meaningful work.

Time-blocking also enhances time management skills by making you aware of how you spend your time. Many people struggle with estimating the time required for tasks and tend to overcommit themselves. Time-blocking forces them to confront their priorities and commitments, enabling them to make intentional decisions about allocating their finite time. By physically blocking out time on a calendar for each obligation, the opportunity cost of saying "yes" becomes tangible, making it easier to say "no" when necessary.

As if that's not enough, time-blocking counteracts perfectionism, a trait that can hinder task progress. Fuzzy timelines and the constant pursuit of perfection can lead to projects dragging on indefinitely. When you impose time limits on tasks, you set clear boundaries and deadlines. This practice helps overcome perfectionist tendencies and encourages you to move forward with the mindset of "good enough." Time-blocking provides a structured approach to completing tasks within designated timeframes, ensuring progress and projects are not unnecessarily prolonged.

It helps you in goal follow-through, too. Research by Drs. Todd Rogers and Katherine L. Milkman support the idea that concrete plans increase the likelihood of following through on intentions. By scheduling specific time blocks for tasks and goals, you create tangible plans as reminders and commitments to take action. Writing down an activity's time, date and location increases the odds of completing it significantly. Time-blocking provides a framework to translate intentions into actionable plans, enabling you to make consistent progress toward your goals.

While time-blocking offers numerous benefits, it's essential to approach it with flexibility and balance. Be careful not to underestimate the time required for tasks by allowing for unforeseen circumstances and staying open to plan adjustments throughout the day. It's also crucial to avoid overscheduling your leisure time; excessive structure can reduce the overall enjoyment of leisure activities. Leave some free time without specific plans to allow for spontaneity and the ability to engage in activities that bring pleasure and relaxation.

In today's modern workplace, one undeniable truth stands out: If you fail to take control of your schedule, it will inevitably take control of you. The demands of meetings, emails, team chat and various "busy work" can easily consume your time, leaving little room for the things you genuinely care about. In this chapter, you have learned about balancing these necessary evils and carving out focused time for your priorities. But this will not always be possible. Sometimes, your plans will fail. Other times, the best-executed schedules will create emergencies you have to give attention to. That's why you need resilience, which will be the topic for the next chapter.

10

BUILD RESILIENCE

Resilience, the ability to adapt and recover in the face of challenges, is a quality that holds immense value in personal and professional lives. Whether you encounter challenges in your career, relationships or daily routines, rebounding from adversity with strength and determination is a hallmark of success. For leaders, resilience becomes even more critical as they navigate the complexities of their roles and guide others through difficult times. Understanding the neuroscience of stress and resilience provides powerful insights into your brain's inner workings and how you can optimize your performance.

Think of your brain as a muscle that can be trained to handle stress and bounce back from setbacks. Just as physical exercise strengthens and conditions your body, your brain's capacity to cope with stress and adversity can be nurtured and developed. This chapter looks into the neuroscience of stress, uncovering the intricate workings of the brain regions involved and discusses techniques to manage stress effectively and cultivate resilience.

STRESS AND ITS IMPACT ON THE BRAIN

Stress is defined as any change that causes physical, emotional or psychological strain. It's a natural response when faced with situations that demand attention or action. While everyone experiences stress to some degree, how you respond to it significantly affects your overall well-being. Understanding what stress feels like and recognizing its signs are the first steps toward effectively managing and mitigating its effects.

Stress often manifests through various emotions and physical sensations that can contribute to irritability, fear, overwork and frustration. You may feel physically exhausted, worn out or unable to cope. However, stress isn't always easy to identify as it can arise from various sources, including seemingly insignificant daily pressures from work, school, family and friends. Even small stresses can accumulate and take a toll on your mind and body.

There are several signs to watch for to determine if stress affects you. Psychological indicators may include difficulty concentrating, excessive worrying, anxiety and trouble remembering. Emotionally, you may experience anger, irritability, moodiness or frustration. On a physical level, stress can manifest as high blood pressure, weight changes, frequent colds or infections, and alterations in the menstrual cycle and libido. Behaviorally, you might notice a decline in self-care practices, lack of time for activities you enjoy or an increased reliance on drugs and alcohol as coping mechanisms.

Stress can be short- or long-term, both of which can lead to various symptoms. However, chronic stress can have severe consequences on the body over time, resulting in long-lasting health effects. Common signs of stress include

- Changes in mood,
- Clammy or sweaty palms,
- Decreased sex drive,
- Diarrhea,
- Difficulty sleeping,
- Digestive problems,
- Dizziness, anxiety,
- Frequent sickness,
- Teeth grinding,
- Headaches,
- Low energy,
- Muscle tension (especially in the neck and shoulders),
- Physical aches and pains,
- Racing heartbeat and trembling.

These physical manifestations serve as signals to take steps to reduce stress and restore balance.

A perceived threat or danger activates the fight-or-flight response — an ancient survival mechanism designed to empower physical fight or escape. Hormones like adrenaline and cortisol are released, leading to increased heart rate, slowed digestion, redirected blood flow to major muscle groups and other autonomic nervous system adjustments that boost energy and strength.

While the fight-or-flight response evolved for situations where physical action was necessary, it's now frequently triggered when neither fighting nor fleeing is appropriate, such as being stuck in traffic or experiencing a stressful day at work. In chronic stress, where the relaxation response does not occur often enough, the body remains in near-constant fight-or-flight activation, leading to potential damage and negative health consequences.

Moreover, stress can contribute to unhealthy habits that further impact your well-being. Many people cope with stress by overeating or resorting to smoking, which can harm the body and exacerbate long-term health problems. It is important to note that not all types of stress are harmful. Different categories of stress that you might experience include:

- **Acute stress** — This is a short-term type of stress commonly encountered daily and can be positive or distressing.
- **Chronic stress** — This type of stress seems unending and inescapable, often arising from factors like a troubled marriage, a demanding job, traumatic experiences or childhood trauma.
- **Episodic acute stress** — This type of stress refers to recurring acute stress where distress pervades daily life, creating ongoing distress.
- **Eustress** — This positive type of stress is associated with stimulating experiences, such as adrenaline surges during activities like skiing or meeting deadlines.

Stress can make it more challenging to cope with daily hassles, strain interpersonal relationships and lead to negative health outcomes. The intricate connection between the mind and body becomes apparent when we examine the impact of stress on our lives. Stress over relationships, finances or living situations can contribute to physical health issues. Conversely, existing health problems, like high blood pressure or diabetes, can also intensify stress levels and affect mental well-being. When the brain experiences high levels of stress, the body responds accordingly.

Acute severe stress, as occurs during a natural disaster or heated argument, can trigger heart attacks, arrhythmias and even sudden death, particularly in individuals with pre-existing heart conditions. Additionally, the emotional toll of stress is equally significant. Prolonged stress can lead to burnout, anxiety disorders and depression. Chronic stress poses a severe threat to health. The overactivation of the autonomic nervous system associated with chronic stress can result in long-term damage to the body.

As earlier mentioned, stress triggers a physiological and neurological response in the body. The fight-or-flight response is activated, releasing hormones like adrenaline and cortisol into the bloodstream. That isn't the only system involved when you're under stress. The amygdala, a key brain region involved in the stress response, stimulates the release of stress-related neurotransmitters when encountering a potential danger, like an oncoming car or a threatening situation. Your sight or hearing sends the information to the amygdala, which plays a role in processing emotions. It swiftly analyzes the images and sounds. If it perceives a threat, the amygdala immediately signals the hypothalamus.

The hypothalamus acts as the brain's command center in charge of involuntary bodily functions like breathing, blood pressure, heartbeat and the dilation or constriction of blood vessels and airways. When the distress signal from the amygdala reaches the hypothalamus, it activates the sympathetic nervous system by sending messages through the autonomic nerves to your adrenal glands.

Here comes an interesting part — the adrenal glands respond by releasing a hormone called epinephrine, also known as adrenaline, into your bloodstream. As epinephrine courses through your body, it brings about several physical changes. Your heart starts racing faster, pumping blood to your muscles, heart and vital organs. Your pulse rate and blood pressure increase, and your breathing becomes more rapid. The small airways in your lungs open wide, allowing you to take in more oxygen with each breath. This extra oxygen is then directed to your brain, enhancing your alertness and sharpening our senses.

But that's not all. Epinephrine also triggers the release of stored blood sugar (glucose) and fats into your bloodstream, providing energy to every body part. All these changes happen in a flash, so quickly that you aren't even aware of them. It's incredibly efficient wiring in your brain that kicks into action before your visual centers fully process what's happening. That's why humans can instinctively leap away from an oncoming car without consciously thinking about it.

Once the initial surge of epinephrine settles down, the hypothalamus activates another stress response component called the HPA axis. This network involves the hypothalamus, pituitary gland and adrenal glands. The HPA axis relies on hormonal signals to keep your sympathetic nervous system, the "gas pedal," engaged. If your brain continues perceiving a threat, the hypothalamus releases corticotropin-releasing hormone (CRH), which travels to the pituitary gland and triggers the release of adrenocorticotropic hormone (ACTH). ACTH then travels to the adrenal glands, prompting them to release cortisol, an essential stress hormone. This keeps your body in a heightened state of alertness and readiness.

Once the threat subsides, cortisol levels decrease and your parasympathetic nervous system, the "brake," kicks in to dampen the stress response and restore balance. Clearly, the brain's stress response is a remarkable system that mobilizes the whole body to deal with threats and challenges. Understanding how it operates can help you navigate and manage stress more effectively, promoting your overall well-being.

UNDERSTANDING RESILIENCE

Resilience, a concept that has fascinated researchers since the 1950s, initially emerged from studies on childhood trauma. Scientists observed children who endured difficult circumstances, yet showed remarkable strength without apparent signs of mental health issues. They labeled this quality "resilience" and set out to understand why some individuals possessed this innate "invulnerability" to stress.

Over time, the definition of resilience has expanded. In 2015, research broadened its scope to encompass a broader ability to adapt to stress and navigate change. Resilience is not limited to those who overcome traumatic childhoods nor does experiencing mental health symptoms imply a lack of resilience. Many psychologists now consider resilience akin to hopefulness or determination and accessible to anyone. It's not an inherent trait but a characteristic developed through experiences.

To put it simply, one must fall before learning how to rise. The learning process equips individuals with the knowledge and skills needed to pick themselves up when they stumble. With each challenge overcome, confidence grows, providing evidence that the person can weather life's storms. Resilience, in essence, refers to the ability to "bounce back" from challenges and setbacks, emerging with a positive outcome despite the trials faced. While interpretations of what constitutes a "hardship" or a "good outcome" may vary, resilience is a blend of persistence, hardiness and flexibility. It implies bending under the weight of adversity but not breaking.

Experts have linked resilience to numerous benefits, including an enhanced social life, improved performance under pressure and a shield against mental health symptoms like depression or anxiety. While not everyone possesses natural resilience, it's indeed possible to cultivate and strengthen it with effort and training. Research in 2018 suggests a correlation between greater resilience and reduced levels of anxiety, stress and depression. Moreover, resilience may offer protection against other mental health concerns, such as post-traumatic stress disorder, rumination and attachment issues. Resilient people tend to exhibit greater ambition, hope, optimism, emotional stability, resourcefulness, delayed gratification and a sense of connection to others and the world at large. Overall, they report higher life satisfaction.

Developing resilience is a complex, individualized process. It involves a combination of internal strengths and external resources, and there is no one-size-fits-all formula for becoming more resilient. Factors such as a person's perspective on — and engagement with — the world, availability and quality of social support and specific coping strategies all contribute to building resilience. It's a journey that unfolds over time, with protective factors established during adolescence contributing to resilience in young adulthood, as evidenced by previous longitudinal studies.

Resilience theory offers valuable insights into the factors that contribute to building resilience. Accordingly, social support plays a vital role in fostering resilience. Supportive social systems, including family, friends, community and organizations, can uplift individuals during times of crisis or trauma. Research confirms that these networks contribute to resilience by offering emotional and practical support.

Self-esteem also plays a role in building resilience. When we have a positive sense of self and confidence in our strengths, we're better equipped to face adversity without succumbing to helplessness. Recent studies have highlighted the close relationship between self-esteem and resilience, emphasizing the importance of nurturing a healthy self-perception. It helps if we have coping skills in our resilience arsenal. The ability to deal with and solve problems empowers us to navigate challenges and overcome hardships. Researchers have found that employing positive coping strategies, such as optimism and sharing, can significantly enhance our resilience compared to nonproductive coping mechanisms.

Resilience theory also fronts effective communication skills as another contributor to resilience. Expressing ourselves clearly and connecting with others help us seek support, mobilize resources and take action. Studies show that people who can interact, show empathy and inspire confidence and trust in others tend to exhibit higher levels of resilience. Finally, emotional regulation helps with resilience. The capacity to manage overwhelming emotions, whether independently or with assistance, enables individuals to maintain focus while overcoming challenges. Studies have linked emotional regulation to improved resilience, emphasizing its role in building the strength to persevere.

Resilience isn't reserved solely for overwhelming moments of adversity. It gradually develops gradually as we encounter various daily stressors. Research on resilience theory highlights resilience as an ongoing process shaped by experiences and responses to daily challenges. You'll understand this better when you consider the "7 Cs" of resilience, a model developed by Dr. Ken Ginsburg to help young people cultivate skills for resilience:

1. **Competence** — Developing the ability to handle situations effectively by acquiring skills and making responsible choices, fostering trust in one's judgments.
2. **Confidence** — True self-confidence is rooted in competence. It grows when people demonstrate their

capabilities in real-life situations, reinforcing their belief in their abilities.

3. **Connection** — Close relationships with family, friends and the community provide a sense of security and belonging, nurturing resilience.

4. **Character** — A fundamental sense of right and wrong enables one to make responsible choices, contribute to society and cultivate self-worth.

5. **Contribution** —- Having a sense of purpose serves as a powerful motivator. Contributing to one's community fosters positive reciprocal relationships and reinforces resilience.

6. **Coping** — Learning to cope with stress effectively equips one to handle adversity and setbacks, bolstering resilience.

7. **Control** — Understanding internal control empowers people to act as problem-solvers instead of victims of circumstance. Control is about recognizing one's ability to influence outcomes, cultivating a sense of capability and confidence.

The 7 Cs highlight the interplay between personal strengths and external resources, irrespective of age. They emphasize the importance of setting high expectations while experiencing unconditional love as ways to help be more resilient. There are different types of resilience, including:

- **Psychological resilience**

Psychological resilience refers to an individual's mental capacity to cope with and adapt to uncertainty, challenges and adversity. It can be likened to "mental fortitude." People with psychological resilience develop coping strategies and skills to maintain calmness and focus during crises. They can bounce back without experiencing long-term negative consequences such as distress and anxiety.

- **Emotional resilience**

How we cope emotionally with stress and adversity differs from person to person. Some are naturally more sensitive to change, while others are more resilient. Emotionally resilient people possess a deep understanding of their emotions and the reasons behind them. They tap into realistic optimism even during a crisis and proactively use internal and external resources to navigate challenging situations. They effectively manage external stressors and handle their emotions in a healthy and positive manner.

- **Physical resilience**

Physical resilience refers to the body's ability to adapt to challenges, maintain stamina and strength, and recover efficiently. It's the human capacity to function and recover when faced with illnesses, accidents and physical demands. Research shows that physical resilience is crucial in healthy aging as people encounter various medical issues and physical stressors.

- **Community resilience**

Community resilience encompasses the collective ability of groups of people to respond to and recover from adverse situations. It pertains to the resilience of communities facing natural disasters, acts of violence, economic hardship and other challenges that impact the entire group.

STRESS MANAGEMENT AND RESILIENCE IN LEADERSHIP

Leading a team in a workplace comes with immense responsibilities. Leaders are trusted by their teams toward professional success while caring about members' well-being. It's a balancing act that requires them to maintain their professional capabilities amidst the demands of their roles. The truth is these demanding workloads can put a significant strain on leaders' mental well-being. The pressure can be overwhelming at times. That's why they must develop efficient coping mechanisms and minimize the negative impacts of stress on their physical and mental health.

To navigate these challenges effectively, leaders equip themselves with stress management and resilience-building knowledge and techniques. That way, they can effectively handle their pressures and create a healthier work environment for everyone involved. Stress management techniques help leaders find balance and maintain their well-being in challenging situations. These strategies enable them to handle stress more efficiently, make informed decisions and maintain overall performance. Resilience-building skills help leaders bounce back from setbacks, adapt to change and cultivate a positive mindset that inspires their team members.

By prioritizing their own mental health and well-being, leaders set an example for team members. They create a culture that values self-care and resilience, allowing their team to thrive and succeed. Ultimately, leaders' well-being directly impacts their teams' well-being, making stress management and resilience-building essential skills for effective leadership. Here are a few ways you can benefit from building resilience:

- **Improved decision-making**

High stress levels can impair your decision-making abilities, leading to poor judgment and suboptimal choices. By practicing effective stress management techniques, you can maintain clarity, reduce the influence of stress on your decision-making process and make more informed decisions that align with organizational goals.

- **Better communication**

Stress can impact communication skills negatively, causing leaders to become short-tempered, dismissive or less attentive to their team's needs. Developing resilience and stress management skills allows you to maintain composure, regulate emotions and communicate more effectively with your team. As an effective leader, you listen actively, provide constructive feedback and foster a supportive and open environment for communication.

- **Increased productivity**

Chronic stress can result in burnout, reducing productivity and the quality of work. Leaders prioritizing effective stress management techniques can maintain their productivity levels and avoid burnout. By implementing time management, delegation and self-care strategies, you can effectively manage stress, stay focused and lead by example.

- **Improved team morale**

A stressed-out leader is likely to hurt team morale and motivation. By developing resilience and stress management skills, you can maintain a positive attitude, even in challenging situations. You create a supportive and inclusive environment that empowers team members, boosts morale and encourages collaboration and engagement.

- **Enhanced creativity and innovation**

Stress can hinder creative thinking and innovation. Leaders who effectively manage stress can maintain an open mind, encouraging creativity and innovation within their teams. By fostering an environment that values diverse perspectives, providing opportunities for brainstorming, and allowing room for experimentation, you can unlock your team's creative potential and drive innovation.

MANAGE STRESS AND BUILD RESILIENCE

There is nothing like practicing mindfulness to help you manage stress and build resilience. The benefits of mindfulness are widely acknowledged and supported by numerous studies. From college students to Marines, research has consistently shown that practicing mindfulness reduces stress and promotes higher levels of well-being. But why does the ability to stay focused on the present moment in a non-judgmental way have such a profound impact on contentment? New research from

India sheds light on one compelling answer — mindfulness cultivates resilience.

In a study conducted by researchers Badri Bajaj and Neerja Pande, published in the journal Personality and Individual Differences, they confirm that mindful individuals exhibit greater psychological resilience. This valuable quality contributes to overall well-being and underlies many of the widely celebrated benefits associated with mindfulness.

The study involved 327 undergraduates — 236 men and 91 women. Participants completed surveys to measure their mindfulness, life satisfaction, emotional state and level of resilience — their ability to cope with difficult situations and bounce back from adversity. Researchers assessed mindfulness through responses to statements such as "I tend to walk quickly to get where I'm going without paying attention to what I experience along the way." Resilience was assessed through self-descriptive statements related to adaptability, focus under pressure and stability in the face of failure.

As expected, the researchers discovered that individuals with higher levels of mindfulness exhibited greater resilience, leading to increased life satisfaction. They observed that resilience is an essential source of subjective well-being and outlined how mindfulness can foster this state of mind. Mindful people can cope with challenging thoughts and emotions without being overwhelmed or shutting down emotionally. They pause and observe their minds, which helps them resist getting caught up in setbacks. In other words, mindfulness weakens the chain of associations that keep people ruminating on their problems or failures, increasing their motivation to try again.

Based on these findings, Bajaj and Pande suggest that universities develop strategies to promote mindfulness among students.

They also suggest that anyone who wishes to build resilience should adopt mindfulness strategies. Mindfulness training is a practical means of enhancing resilience and cultivating other positive personality characteristics like optimism, zest and patience. Mindfulness is characterized by an intentional, non-judgmental focus on the present moment. It encompasses awareness, focus, acceptance and observation. Some mindfulness techniques to get you started include:

- **Mindful breathing**

Mindful breathing is a valuable tool to bring yourself back to the present moment, especially in times of stress. By combining mindfulness and breathing techniques, you cultivate awareness of your experiences and embrace each moment to its fullest potential. But how does this work in practice, you may wonder? Breath is the essence of life. Through inhaling, you provide oxygen to your cells, while exhaling allows you to release waste products like carbon dioxide. Different breathing techniques have distinct effects on your body. For instance, rhythmic breathing helps to balance the nervous system.

Mindful breathing activates the parasympathetic nervous system, known as the body's "rest and digest" system. This activation decreases heart rate and blood pressure, helping alleviate anxiety along the way. Mindful breathing has shown promise in reducing burnout, cynicism, emotional exhaustion and stress. For those dealing with depression, practicing mindful breathing can help reduce negative automatic thoughts and pave the way for an improved mood.

There are many ways you can incorporate mindful breathing into your routine. Start by practicing it during your morning ritual to relieve muscle stiffness and tension in the back or if you prefer, practice it at the end of your day. Here's a simple exercise: Start bystanding and then bending forward from the waist with slightly bent knees, allowing your arms to hang close to the floor. Inhale slowly and deeply as you gradually return to standing, rolling up and lifting your head last. Hold your breath for a few seconds in this upright position. As you exhale slowly, return to the original position by bending forward from the waist. Pay attention to how you feel at the end of the exercise, observing any changes or sensations that arise.

- **Body scan meditation**

Sometimes, people get so consumed by stress that they fail to recognize the physical discomfort it brings — like headaches, back and shoulder pain, and overall muscle tension — as connected with their emotional state. To address this, body scan meditation offers a powerful way to release physical tension that often goes unnoticed. Systematically scanning your body brings awareness to every part's aches, pains, tension or discomfort. The purpose isn't to eliminate the pain but to understand and learn from it, enabling you to better manage it.

Consistently practice body scan meditation, ideally daily or even multiple times a day, to enjoy its various mental and physical health benefits. Research indicates that one of the primary advantages of body scan meditation is stress reduction, which can lead to physical improvements such as reduced inflammation, fatigue and insomnia. This practice helps break the self-perpetuating cycle of physical and psychological tension.

Like all forms of meditation, body scan should be simple. To get started, find comfort. Ideally, lie down, especially if you're doing the body scan meditation before sleep. If lying down isn't possible or comfortable, sitting in a comfortable position works, too. Once you're situated, take deep breaths. Allow your breath to slow down, focusing on breathing from your belly instead of your chest. Let your abdomen expand and contract with each breath. If you notice your shoulders rising and falling, redirect your focus to breathing from your belly, envisioning a balloon inflating and deflating within your abdomen.

Once you settle into a breathing rhythm, direct attention to your feet. Gradually shift your attention to your feet, noticing the sensations within them. If you encounter any pain, acknowledge it with any accompanying thoughts or emotions, then gently breathe through it. Be sure to breathe into the tension. Whenever you come across uncomfortable sensations, direct your attention to them. Breathe into those areas and observe what happens. Visualize the tension leaving your body with each breath, dissipating into the air. Proceed to the next area when you feel ready.

Continue this practice by gradually moving up from your feet to the top of your head. Take note of how you feel and where you hold stress. If you encounter any tightness, pain or pressure, continue breathing into those sensations. This can help you release tension in the present moment and increase awareness in the future, enabling you to remove it more effectively. Regular body scan meditation fosters a deeper connection between your mind and body, promoting relaxation, self-awareness and overall well-being.

- **Loving kindness meditation**

Loving kindness meditation is a widely practiced technique for self-care that's proven effective in enhancing well-being and reducing stress. Regular practitioners expand their capacity for forgiveness, connection with others, self-acceptance and more.

Engaging in this technique requires a willingness to extend kindness to yourself and others, which can be challenging at first. It takes time and practice to open yourself to receive self-love or to send it to others.

During a loving kindness meditation session, the focus is on directing benevolent and loving energy toward yourself and others. Traditional meditation has numerous documented benefits, and this specific style requires dedication and persistence. There are various approaches to practicing this meditation, each rooted in different Buddhist traditions. However, they all share the same core psychological process involving the cultivation of kind intentions towards specific targets, including oneself and others.

The following is a simple, yet effective technique for loving kindness meditation that you can try:

1. Set aside quiet time for yourself, even just a few minutes. Find a comfortable sitting position, close your eyes, relax your muscles and take a few deep breaths.
2. Visualize yourself experiencing complete physical and emotional well-being along with inner peace. Imagine feeling an unconditional love for yourself, expressing gratitude for all you are and recognizing that you're perfect just the way you are. Focus on this sense of inner peace and envision exhaling tension while inhaling feelings of love.
3. Repeat three or four positive and reassuring phrases to yourself. Here are some examples, but feel free to create your own:

- *May I be happy.*
- *May I be safe.*

- *May I be healthy, peaceful and strong.*
- *May I give and receive appreciation today.*

Allow yourself to bask for a few moments in the warmth and self-compassion generated by these phrases. If your mind wanders, gently guide your attention to these feelings of loving kindness. Allow emotions to envelop you. At this point, you can either maintain your focus on self-compassion or gradually shift your attention to loved ones in your life. Start with someone you are emotionally close to, such as your spouse, child, parent or best friend. Feel and acknowledge the gratitude and love you have for them. Stay with that feeling. You may choose to repeat the reassuring phrases.

Once you have immersed yourself in loving feelings for that person, gradually expand your awareness to other significant individuals in your life, one by one. Envision each person experiencing perfect well-being and inner peace. Then broaden your focus to include other family, friends, neighbors, acquaintances or people worldwide. You may find it helpful to include those with whom you have conflicts; this can help in the process of forgiveness or reaching greater peace. When you feel your meditation is complete, gently open your eyes. Remember that you can revisit the beautiful feelings you cultivated throughout the day. Internalize the experience of loving kindness meditation and reconnect with those emotions by shifting your focus and taking a few deep breaths.

Resilience-building is an essential skill for leaders in a dynamic world. Leaders who possess resilience are better equipped to navigate uncertainty, adapt to change and overcome obstacles. They withstand adversity while inspiring and guiding their teams through difficult times. In this chapter, you've explored various strategies and practices leaders employ to cultivate resilience. You've learned about the effects of stress and how it hinders leadership.

The next chapter will focus on the sustained growth you can reach through resilience. It will answer the question, "How can leaders sustain adopting new skills to ensure continuous growth?"

11

SUSTAINED GROWTH

I n the post-industrial revolution world, organizations face the constant need for change and adaptation. Whether adopting new technologies, restructuring operations or transforming corporate cultures, change initiatives have become a necessity. Organizations must either change or die. However, the reality is that successfully implementing and sustaining change is an ongoing challenge for leaders, too. Studies show that a staggering 70% of all change initiatives fail to achieve desired outcomes.

This chapter discusses the complex dynamics of sustained growth, focusing on the barriers that hinder the integration and longevity of new leadership skills in everyday life. It explores the reasons behind the high failure rate of change initiatives and offers strategies that foster sustainable change. Change implementation requires more than just a blueprint or a set of guidelines. It demands a deep understanding of the factors that impede progress and a proactive approach to overcoming obstacles. This chapter addresses the common barriers leaders and organizations encounter when striving to integrate change.

THE BARRIERS TO INTEGRATING NEW SKILLS

Imagine a company operating in the heart of an urban land-scape, set in its traditional ways and hesitant to embrace sustainable practices. This organization could be a long-standing global enterprise that has etched its presence in the city for decades or a local business with deep roots in the community. It might even mirror an experience you've encountered personally. What key barriers prohibit the business from adopting more sustainable practice?

For starters, habits are difficult to break. As human beings, we are creatures of habit, and over time, certain behaviors become deeply ingrained in daily routines and decision-making processes. These habits can be so automatic that even when we acquire new skills or knowledge that offer more effective ways of doing things, we may still find ourselves reverting to the old, familiar ways. This phenomenon occurs because habits form through repetition and reinforcement. They create well-worn neural pathways in the brain, making defaulting to established patterns easier than consciously adopting new behaviors. Breaking these entrenched habits requires conscious effort, willpower and consistency in practicing the new behavior until it becomes more automatic and overpowers the old routine.

Perhaps the organization's leaders know the environmental benefits and efficiency of adopting more sustainable practices. But if their long-standing habits are deeply rooted in non-sustainable behaviors, overcoming the inertia and making necessary changes can be difficult. A person, for example, might know that using public transportation or cycling to work is better for the environment than driving a car. Still, if they've been commuting by car for years, the ingrained habit of driving may persist despite the knowledge. Similarly, a business may recognize the advantages of adopting eco-friendly manufacturing processes. Still, if its established methods have been in place for a long time, leaders may struggle to shift away from them. Overcoming old habits requires a concerted effort to rewire the brain's automatic responses. It also requires patience and understanding that breaking old habits and embracing sustainable change is a process that may take time and consistent practice.

It doesn't help your efforts if you're overwhelmed with multiple tasks or responsibilities, making it challenging to prioritize and integrate new skills into your routine. When people find themselves juggling duties and obligations as leaders often do, allocating time and mental energy to learning and incorporating new skills can be challenging. The demands of daily life, including work, family responsibilities, social commitments and personal obligations, can leave little room to learn and practice new skills. The limited available time may lead to postponing or neglecting skill development altogether. Not only that but feeling overwhelmed can result in mental fatigue, leaving you with depleted cognitive resources. When the mind is preoccupied with multiple responsibilities, focusing on learning new skills and retaining information effectively is harder.

When this happens where you don't have support from friends, family or colleagues, it gets even more complicated. As people, we're highly influenced by the social norms and behaviors of others. If others don't value or encourage the skills we're trying to integrate, we may feel pressured to conform to prevailing non-sustainable behaviors. This social pressure can discourage us from embracing sustainable change, fearing that we'll stand out or be perceived negatively by others. Besides, supportive friends, family, or colleagues can provide motivation and encouragement. When we receive positive reinforcement for our choices, it strengthens our commitment and enthusiasm for continuing those behaviors. Without such support, we may struggle to find the motivation to sustain our efforts.

Hesitation to try new skills — for fear of failure or mistakes —is another significant barrier to lasting change. This fear is deeply ingrained in human psychology and can prevent an individual from venturing into new territory, embracing change and pursuing personal or professional growth. People tend to find comfort in what they know and are familiar with. Trying new skills requires stepping outside this comfort zone, which can be uncomfortable and anxiety-inducing. An added pressure is the fear of being judged by others when we don't immediately excel at a new skill. We may worry about how our peers, colleagues or family members will see us if we make mistakes during the learning process. Those with high expectations for themselves may fear that trying something new will lead to imperfection or failure. Fear of not meeting the unrealistic standards deters them from integrating new skills.

STRATEGIES FOR SUSTAINABLE CHANGE

If the odds seem so stacked against us, how do we start to live out the new knowledge and skills for lasting change? Successfully integrating and sustaining newfound skills requires planning, consistency and commitment.

- **Set clear goals.**

Take some time to identify specific goals that resonate with you. Ask yourself, "What do I want to achieve through learning and applying these new skills?" Being specific will give you a clear direction and purpose. It could be anything from advancing your career, starting a new hobby or improving your overall knowledge.

Having clear goals will help you stay motivated throughout your learning journey. It's easier to keep pushing forward when you know what you're working towards, even when challenges arise. As you tick off those goals one by one, the sense of accomplishment will boost your confidence and keep you going. Imagine how rewarding it'll be to look back and see the progress you've made by sticking to your goals. It's like scoring points in a game, only this time it's your real-life achievements! You can use the following pointers to make those goals more achievable:

- **Tie them to a "why."**

Connecting your goals to a meaningful "why" is crucial to reaching them. When you understand the purpose behind your actions, staying focused and avoiding distractions becomes much easier. So, take a moment to figure out why you want to achieve those goals. Understanding your purpose will help you gain clarity, articulate your ideas and prioritize what truly matters.

- **Break them down.**

Instead of pursuing one massive goal, why not follow business coach Allison Walsh's advice and embrace a 90-day sprint? Think of it like a series of smaller, achievable goals that add to your bigger vision. For example, if you plan to read 50 books this year, break it down into about 10 books for the next 90 days. Create a plan to get there, like spending the first week picking out exciting books and then committing to reading two chapters a day.

- **Plan "buffer time" for your goals.**

One researcher points out that we tend to overestimate our capabilities and underestimate external factors that can affect us. To avoid this trap, add extra time to your deadlines to account for unexpected delays. Use technology tools or find an accountability partner to keep you on track and focused on your journey.

- **Choose continuation over improvement.**

It helps to shift your perspective from self-improvement to self-acceptance. Self-acceptance embraces what you've already started and then builds upon it. Instead of judging yourself for not being perfect, see your goals as a continuation of your progress so far. This mindset will make your journey feel more comfortable, safe and successful.

- **Move on from past failures.**

Everyone goes through ups and downs. Don't dwell on past failures but instead learn from them. Stay positive, believe in yourself and remember that setbacks are just stepping stones on your path to success.

- **Create a plan.**

Most people start a new "habit" but quit a few days later. To combat this, develop a detailed plan that outlines the steps you need to integrate and sustain the new skills. The plan should include specific actions you can take to incorporate the new skills into your daily routine. You can use the following nine-step process to build positive habits that become part of your daily routine. It works because it focuses on small, incremental steps:

1. Focus on one new skill.

One common obstacle to forming new habits is ego depletion — the diminished capacity to regulate thoughts, feelings and actions. It impacts our ability to create habits because our willpower spreads thin across various aspects of life. That's why only one skill at a time is crucial. By doing so, you can concentrate your willpower on mastering that one skill, thus increasing your chances of success. Ask yourself: "What one new skill do I want to learn?" Identify it clearly and understand how it will make you a better leader. The goal is to work on that skill until you've mastered it before moving on to the next.

2. Commit to at least 30 days.

Leadership excellence doesn't happen overnight. Some researchers say it takes 21 days to create a new habit. Others say it takes 66 days. The length of time varies from person to person and habit to habit. Dedicate yourself to practicing your new skill consistently for at least 30 days. Embrace the journey and be patient with yourself. Rome wasn't built in a day and neither will your leadership prowess.

3. Anchor the skill to an established routine.

To make this skill a part of your daily life, anchor it to an existing routine. Whether during your morning routine, before meetings or after work, find a time that fits seamlessly into your day. This way, practicing your skill becomes second nature. A habit shouldn't rely on motivation, temporary desire or fads. Anchoring it into something you already do increases the chances you'll keep doing it.

4. Focus on the tiny skills that make up the bigger skill.

Leadership excellence is a combination of various minor skills. Break down the more extensive skill into smaller, manageable parts. Focus on mastering one before moving on to the next. Remember, excellence lies in attention to detail. For example, suppose the "big skill" is becoming a great communicator. In that case, the tiny skills may include practicing active listening, being mindful of your posture and facial expressions and using positive language, which you could master one by one.

5. Don't break the chain.

Create a chain of consistent practice days. Put an "X" on your calendar each day you practice your new skill. The goal is simple: Don't break the chain! Seeing your progress visually will motivate you to keep going.

6. Plan for obstacles and challenges.

Life happens, and obstacles may come your way. Anticipate challenges and have a plan to tackle them. Whether it's a busy schedule or unexpected events, find creative solutions to keep your practice on track.

7. Track your new skill.

Keep a record of your progress. Journal your experiences, note your improvements and write down the challenges you faced. Reflecting on your journey will give you valuable insights and help you stay on course.

8. Reward milestones.

Celebrate your achievements, no matter how small. Every milestone you reach is a step towards leadership excellence. Treat yourself to something meaningful or indulge in a bit of self-appreciation. Positive reinforcement goes a long way in sustaining motivation.

9. Build a new identity.

To truly integrate the skill into your leadership style, embrace it as part of who you are. Visualize yourself as the leader you aspire to be and let that image guide your actions. Embodying the skill will make it a natural extension of yourself.

MORE TIPS FOR SUCCESSFUL HABITS

- **Practice consistently.**

Practicing your new skills every day, no matter how briefly, can be incredibly powerful and beneficial. This is because consistency breeds mastery. Repetition is critical to mastering any skill. Daily practice, even for just a short period, reinforces neural pathways in your brain related to that skill. This consistent practice helps you retain information and improve your performance over time.

The daily practice also creates momentum. It keeps you engaged and motivated as you see incremental progress day by day. The sense of accomplishment from each small practice session can fuel your desire to continue and improve. It also develops muscle memory. Regular practice helps your body and mind become more familiar with the movements and actions required, making them more automatic and precise.

- **Get feedback.**

Though sometimes intimidating, feedback is an invaluable tool for personal growth and development. Seeking feedback from others allows us to gain insights into our progress, helps identify areas for improvement and ultimately leads to refining our skills and building confidence. Feedback acts as a mirror, reflecting our actions and behaviors. It provides an external perspective that we may not always perceive ourselves, shedding light on strengths and weaknesses. This valuable insight is essential for fostering growth and driving us toward success.

Receiving feedback enables us to gauge our progress accurately. This is especially necessary when we're learning a new skill. It allows us to measure how far we've come and provides benchmarks to set new goals. Without feedback, we may be adrift, unaware of our position on the path to success. If the feedback is constructive, it provides us with specific areas that require improvement. It highlights areas where we might be faltering or overlooking growth opportunities. By embracing this feedback, we gain the advantage of self-awareness and the chance to address our weaknesses directly.

Essentially, the feedback loop acts as a continuous cycle of improvement. Armed with constructive criticism, we can refine our skills. Whether honing our presentation abilities, mastering public speaking or fine-tuning our communication skills, feedback guides us towards becoming better leaders. The iterative process of learning and adapting shapes us into competent leaders. However, seeking feedback requires humility and an open mind. It may be uncomfortable to face our imperfections, but acknowledging them is a significant step toward improvement. Commit to accepting feedback with gratitude. You will reap the rewards for it.

- **Celebrate successes.**

As we integrate new skills, it's essential to celebrate every success, no matter how small or seemingly insignificant it may seem. Acknowledging progress isn't merely a pat on the back; it's a powerful tool to keep us motivated and committed to the journey. Celebrating our successes, irrespective of their magnitude, helps us keep a positive mindset. It's easy to overlook small achievements, dismissing them as inconsequential. However, these seemingly minor triumphs contribute significantly to the overall progress. By celebrating them, we foster an atmosphere of continuous growth and encouragement.

When we celebrate our successes, we recognize the progress we've made. Acknowledgment is a powerful motivator. It reminds us that our efforts are bearing fruit and that we're on the right track. The sense of accomplishment we experience reinforces our dedication to the process, propelling us forward with renewed enthusiasm. It helps us cultivate commitment. Each celebration serves as a reaffirmation of our belief in our capabilities. As we commemorate our achievements, we become more committed to the journey, willing to face challenges head-on, and more likely to navigate obstacles with resilience.

The act of celebrating successes aligns with the concept of a growth mindset. Rather than solely focusing on results, we acknowledge the value of progress and learning from each step of the journey. Embracing a growth mindset allows us to view challenges as opportunities and setbacks as stepping stones toward improvement. It creates a positive cycle of motivation and achievement. As we acknowledge our progress, our motivation grows, leading us to set higher goals and strive for greater accomplishments. The more we celebrate, the more we achieve and the more motivated we become to achieve even more. Some ways you can celebrate your successes include:

- **Practice self-care.**

Treating yourself to self-care activities is a wonderful way to celebrate your achievements. Whether indulging in a spa day, taking a long walk in nature or simply enjoying a moment of quiet reflection, self-care rejuvenates your mind and body, preparing you for the next exciting challenge.

- **Spend time with those you love.**

Share your success with the people who matter most to you. Spending quality time with loved ones, friends and family allows you to bask in the joy together and creates lasting memories. Celebrating with loved ones strengthens your support network and reminds you of the incredible people who have been by your side on your journey.

- **Express gratitude.**

Express your gratitude to those who supported and believed in you. Send a heartfelt thank-you note or a small token of appreciation to mentors, friends or colleagues who contributed to your success. Showing your appreciation reinforces positive relationships and nurtures a sense of community.

- **Engage in creative activities.**

Channel your creativity to commemorate your achievements. Create a vision board with future goals, paint a picture inspired by your success or write a journal entry reflecting on your journey. Engaging in creative activities fosters introspection and helps you connect with your inner passions.

- **Practice gratitude.**

Take a moment to be grateful for all that you have accomplished. Celebrating success with gratitude keeps you grounded, reminding you of your progress and blessings in life. Gratitude cultivates a positive mindset, enabling you to approach future challenges with optimism.

- **Embrace spontaneity.**

Celebrate your success with spontaneity. Allow yourself to enjoy unexpected pleasures, like going on a last-minute trip, trying a new activity or treating yourself to a special meal. Embracing spontaneity brings an element of excitement and joy to your celebrations.

- **Use your success as fuel.**

Use your success as motivation to keep pushing forward. Celebrate your accomplishments, but let them also serve as a reminder of what you can achieve. Allow your success to fuel your ambition and determination to reach even greater heights.

- **Stay accountable.**

Integrating and sustaining new skills is an empowering journey that requires dedication and discipline. Finding someone to hold you accountable can make a substantial difference in achieving your goals. Accountability guides us, keeping us committed to our goals and responsible for our actions. When we have someone to hold us accountable, whether a friend, mentor or coach, we're more likely to remain focused and disciplined in pursuing our newfound skills. This external support system provides valuable feedback, encouragement and guidance throughout our growth journey. To stay accountable:

- **Work with an accountability partner.**

One of the most effective ways to stay accountable is by enlisting an accountability partner. This needs to be someone who is invested in your success and is willing to check in on your progress regularly. They may share similar goals or have expertise in the area you're striving to improve. Practice sharing your achievements and challenges with them to gain a sense of responsibility to keep moving forward even when obstacles arise.

- **Share your goals publicly.**

Making your goals public can be a powerful motivator. Share the skills you hope to develop with friends, family or on social media platforms. Going public adds an extra layer of accountability as you become more conscious of the expectations others have for you. The support and encouragement from your network can spur you on during challenging times, creating a positive environment for growth.

- **Change your environment.**

Our environment greatly influences our habits and actions. To hold yourself accountable:

- Consider choosing surroundings to support your goals.
- Create a dedicated workspace or establish a daily routine that encourages practicing your new skills.
- Surround yourself with inspirational material and like-minded individuals who share your passion for self-improvement.

A conducive environment will make it easier to stay focused and committed to your journey.

- **Embrace failure.**

The path to integrating new leadership skills is paved with challenges and sometimes failure. Rather than fearing failure, embracing it as an integral part of the learning process is essential for personal growth and leadership development. Failure is an inevitable part of any learning journey, including developing leadership skills. As we explore uncharted territories and push ourselves to new limits, missteps and challenges will arise. Understanding that failure is a natural part of the process allows us to reframe our perspective, recognizing it not as a dead-end but as an opportunity for growth.

When you face setbacks or make mistakes, don't be discouraged. Instead, view them as valuable opportunities to learn and improve. Failure gives us invaluable insights and lessons that success alone cannot provide. Embracing our mistakes with a growth mindset empowers us to turn adversity into progress, fostering resilience and perseverance. Besides, every failure, no matter its size, carries hidden lessons. Reflect on the experience and ask yourself what you can learn from it. Identify areas where you can improve, understand the root causes of the failure and strategize ways to avoid similar pitfalls in the future.

Integrating new leadership skills into our daily lives is a transformative journey that requires dedication, perseverance and an unwavering commitment to personal growth. Throughout this chapter, you've explored the key elements contributing to successful integration: setting clear goals, staying accountable, celebrating successes, embracing failure and seeking feedback from others. These principles can serve as guiding beacons on your path to becoming effective and influential leaders.

As you navigate the complexities of leadership, it's crucial to remember that growth is a continuous process. Each day presents an opportunity to build on your skills, refine your approaches and learn from successes and setbacks. Remain steadfast in your pursuit of growth and be willing to face challenges head-on. Your commitment to personal development will elevate your leadership abilities and inspire those around you to thrive and excel.

KNOWLEDGE IS POWER!

To walk with like-minded leaders, we need to create more...
and you can make that happen.

Simply by sharing your honest opinion of this book and a little
about your own leadership journey, you'll show new readers
how neuroscience plays a critical role in exceptional leadership.
Please help us by contributing with a book review on Amazon:
Amazon.com/review/create-review?&asin=B0CLGTPV7F

JUST ONE CLICK!

Thank you for your support. May your learning continue and
your leadership reach new heights. Here is my website: www.
lcgnow.com

CONCLUSION

As you finish this book and this journey through the fascinating world of neuroscience and leadership, you've equipped yourself with a wealth of knowledge and practical insights to become an exceptional leader. Each chapter has revealed the intricate workings of the brain and how it impacts your behavior, mindset and decision-making, ultimately shaping your leadership abilities. In Chapter 1, you learned that the brain is the foundation of leadership, and understanding its anatomy and physiology is crucial for mastering your potential. In Chapter 2, you explored the power of the mind and the concept of neuroplasticity, empowering you to embrace a growth mindset, continually evolving and adapting to new challenges.

Next, you learned the importance of emotional intelligence in leadership, emphasizing the significance of self-awareness and empathy for effective leadership, and you were guided on staying focused, getting valuable techniques to enhance attention and concentration along the way, enabling you to lead with clarity and precision. Chapter 5 delved into enhancing memory and retention, equipping you with strategies to optimize learning and recall, which are essential for making informed decisions as a leader. Then, you sparked your creativity and innovation, understanding how to harness the power of creative thinking to tackle complex challenges with fresh perspectives.

In Chapter 7, you explored the science of making the right call, emphasizing the significance of effective decision-making and problem-solving in leadership. In Chapter 8, you learned how to communicate and maximize your productivity in chapter 9. Chapters 10 and 11 helped you to build resilience and sustain your growth.

You've learned the ways the mind affects how you lead, whether it's in your ability to bounce back from adversity or in your desire to lead with optimal productivity. You've reflected on the barriers to integrating new skills and discovered strategies for sustainable change. You have everything you need to unlock your leadership potential.

Note From the Author

The principles and skills discussed in this book have worked for a long time. One of my clients, a young minority leader struggling to gain respect from her team, was able to change that by incorporating lessons learned in this book. Through coaching, could identify and work on her communication skills, which improved team dynamics, project outcomes and respect from coworkers. Another client, a director at a tech startup, improves his time management and productivity skills, leading to a promotion as vice president. These are just a few examples of leaders who have become better equipped to confidently lead their teams and make strategic business decisions.

Their stories could be yours. I hope the wisdom gained from this book becomes the cornerstone of your leadership journey, enabling you to lead with empathy, vision and resilience.

Embrace the power of the brain and the boundless potential within you, and I hope you find fulfillment in your pursuit of excellence as a leader. Remember, the journey toward sustained growth never truly ends; it only evolves and expands with every step we take.

If you'd like to walk with like-minded leaders who have transformed their lives and careers by applying the strategies outlined in this book, join our community so that we can continue to learn, grow and unlock our full potential. While you're at it, let someone know how you found this book by leaving a review. Here's to all the best on your leadership journey!

ABOUT THE AUTHOR

Marlene Gonzalez is the founder and the president of Life coaching group LLC. focusing on Leadership development and executive coaching. She passionately pursues one vision- "To advance, develop and promote minority leaders." She is a renowned executive coach and facilitator. She is the author of the coaching series Leadership Wizard; "Number 1 New Release book in the Education and Leadership category". Her book series are available o Amazon and specializes in transformational leadership topics such as:

- *Leadership Wizard. The Nine Dimensions. Unlock the Leader in You. The Discipline of Coaching Yourself to Fearlessly Lead, Influence, Inspire and Empower Others.*
- *Assertive Wizard. How To Boost Confidence, Get Your Message Across, And Speak with Impact.*
- *Change Wizard. Master The Art of Leading Change and Working Together for a Common Purpose.*
- *Confident Wizard.* Turn Self Doubt into Confidence: The Ultimate Guide to Lead With Authenticity, Purpose, and Resilience.
- *Conflicted.* Connecting the 4 Phases of Conflict Management Through Logic and Emotion.

Once you master these and many other topics she covers, you can transform your life and become a more successful leader. In addition, you will find that her books have a straight-to-the-point approach and easy to implement actions. She is passionate about sharing her insights and resources on transformational leadership through a combination of Insights Discovery, the psychology of C. G. Jung, her corporate career experience, and her professional coaching expertise.

González held many executive corporate positions in the US, Europe, and Latin America. She is the former Senior Director of Global Training, Learning, and Development for McDonald's Corporation. Marlene holds a BS, an Executive MBA, PAG, and a graduate diploma on managerial Issues in the global enterprise from Thunderbird University. She also has a Professional Certified Coaching credential from the International Coaching Federation, a global partnership with Insights Discovery based in the United Kingdom, and a neuroscience certification for business from the Massachusetts Institute of Technology, MIT, Sloan School of Management. She is pursuing her Doctorate in Business Administration focus on Organizational Neuroscience from the Monarch Business School in Switzerland. This shows her commitment to staying up to date with the latest research and advancements in leadership development, executive coaching and team dynamics. In her free time, Marlene enjoys cooking, reading, trekking, and exploring the world for new experiences with her husband, Carlos. They reside in Chicago, Illinois.

REFERENCES

A surprising new source of attention in the brain — News. (Jan. 20, 2021). News. https://www.rockefeller.edu/news/26994-new-attention-area-in-brain-discovered/

Ackerman, C.E., MA. (2023). What is neuroplasticity? A psychologist explains [+14 tools]. *PositivePsychology.com.* https://positivepsychology.com/neuroplasticity/

Baxter, M.G., & Croxson, P.L. (2012). Facing the role of the amygdala in emotional information processing. *Proceedings of the National Academy of Sciences of the United States of America, 109*(52), 21180–21181. https://doi.org/10.1073/pnas.1219167110

Beth. (2020, November 1). *5 inspirational quotes & pioneers of Neuroplasticity.* Home. https://www.bethkendall.com/blog/5-inspirational-quotes-and-pioneers-in-neuroplasticity

Boston University. (June 25, 2019). *How does the human brain store and retrieve memories? | The Brink | Boston University.* https://www.bu.edu/articles/2016/human-brain-store-retrieve-memories

Brain anatomy and how the brain works. (July 14, 2021). Johns Hopkins Medicine. https://www.hopkinsmedicine.org/health/conditions-and-diseases/anatomy-of-the-brain

Carrots, P. (2022, March 4). *Growth mindset: The science of failure and neuroplasticity.* James Egerton. https://jamesegerton.wordpress.com/2021/02/27/growth-mindset-the-science-of-failure-and-neuroplasticity/

Dranitsaris-Hilliard, H. (n.d.). Brain and leadership behavior: Self-awareness begins with getting to know your brain. *www.linkedin.com.* https://www.linkedin.com/pulse/brain-leadership-behavior-self-awareness-begins-know-heather/

Felton, A. (Sept. 8, 2022). *Limbic system: What to know.* WebMD. https://www.webmd.com/brain/limbic-system-what-to-know

Glukhovskyy, A. (June 16, 2023). Leading with a growth mindset: Lead like the best. *GrowthTribe.* https://growthtribe.io/blog/leading-with-a-growth-mindset

GoodTherapy | Prefrontal cortex. (n.d.). https://www.goodtherapy.org/blog/psychpedia/prefrontal-cortex

GrapeSEED. (Sept. 30, 2020). *How a growth mindset and neuroplasticity boosts learning.* https://region.grapeseed.com/us/blog/how-a-growth-mindset-and-neuroplasticity-boosts-learning/

Growth mindset: Why it's needed for successful leadership. (n.d.). https://blog.growthinstitute.com/the-edge/growth-mindset-successful-leadership

Gupta, S. (2023). Focus: Benefits and characteristics. *Verywell Mind.* https://www.verywellmind.com/focus-characteristics-benefits-and-drawbacks-5323828

Halber, D. (n.d.). *The anatomy of emotions.* https://www.brainfacts.org/thinking-sensing-and-behaving/emotions-stress-and-anxiety/2018/the-anatomy-of-emotions-090618

Heid, M. (Sept. 19, 2018). Does thinking burn calories? Here's what the science says. *Time.* https://time.com/5400025/does-thinking-burn-calories/

How the brain processes emotions. (March 31, 2016). MIT News | Massachusetts Institute of Technology. https://news.mit.edu/2016/brain-processes-emotions-mental-illness-depression-0331

Ivy Lee Method — Workflowy guide. (n.d.). https://workflowy.com/systems/ivy-lee-method/

Kizer, K. (2023). 35+ Powerful leadership statistics [2023]: Things all aspiring leaders should know. *Zippia.* https://www.zippia.com/advice/leadership-statistics/#:~:text=Only%2010%25%20of%20people%20are,%24366%20billion%20that's%20spent%20globally.

Mayfield brain & spine. (n.d.). MAYFIELD. https://mayfieldclinic.com/pe-anat brain.htm

Moawad, H., MD. (Nov. 14, 2020). How the brain processes emotions. *Neurology Live.* https://www.neurologylive.com/view/how-brain-processes-emotions

Nelson, A. (Nov. 29, 2022). *The basis of leadership is born in the brain | Neuroscience In Business.* Hppy. https://gethppy.com/leadership/basis-of-leadership-neuroscience

@neurochallenged. (n.d.). *Know your brain: cingulate cortex.* @Neurochallenged. https://neuroscientificallychallenged.com/posts/know-your-brain-cingulate-cortex

Ng, B. (2018). The neuroscience of growth mindset and intrinsic motivation. *Brain Sciences, 8*(2), 20. https://doi.org/10.3390/brainsci8020020

OpenStaxCollege. (Feb. 14, 2014). *Parts of the brain involved with memory.* Pressbooks. https://pressbooks-dev.oer.hawaii.edu/psychology/chapter/parts-of-the-brain-involved-with-memory/

Post page. (n.d.). https://stratleader.net/sli-blog/neurocoaching

Professional, C.C.M. (n.d.). *Brain.* Cleveland Clinic. https://my.clevelandclinic.org/health/body/22638-brain

Publisher, A.R. a. R.O.O. (Oct. 26, 2015). *3.2 Our brains control our thoughts, feelings, and behavior.* Pressbooks. https://open.lib.umn.edu/intropsyc/chapter/3-2-our-brains-control-our-thoughts-feelings-and-behavior/

Seladi-Schulman, J., PhD. (July 24, 2018). *What part of the brain controls emotions?*

Healthline. https://www.healthline.com/health/what-part-of-the-brain-controls-emotions

Silver, N. (May 27, 2022). *Understanding the connection between a growth mindset and neuroplasticity.* Healthline. https://www.healthline.com/health/growth-mindset-neuroplasticity

The connection of attention, focus and intent | Gloveworx. (n.d.). Gloveworx. https://www.gloveworx.com/blog/connection-attention-focus-and-intent/

The essential role of a growth mindset and neuroplasticity in facilitating lifelong learning. (n.d.). https://www.lifesnotebook.com/post/essential-role-growth-mindset-neuroplasticity-facilitating-lifelong-learning

The Leadership Institute. (2019). Mastering the 3 areas of focused leadership. *The Leadership Institute.* https://www.theleadershipinstitute.com.au/2019/11/mastering-the-3-areas-of-focused-leadership/

Touronis, V. (2022). How to develop a growth mindset. *My Online Therapy.* https://myonlinetherapy.com/how-to-develop-a-growth-mindset/

Training Industry, Inc. (2019). Understanding our brains: Essential knowledge for 21st-century leaders. *Training Industry.* https://trainingindustry.com/articles/leadership/understanding-our-brains-essential-knowledge-for-21st-century-leaders/

Training Industry, Inc. (2022). How the brain learns. *Training Industry.* https://trainingindustry.com/articles/content-development/how-the-brain-learns/

Types of memory. (Aug. 31, 2022). Queensland Brain Institute — University of Queensland. https://qbi.uq.edu.au/brain-basics/memory/types-memory

Where are memories stored in the brain? (July 23, 2018). Queensland Brain Institute - University of Queensland. https://qbi.uq.edu.au/brain-basics/memory/where-are-memories-stored

Why a growth mindset is crucial for leadership — McCracken. (n.d.). https://www.mccrackenalliance.com/blog/why-a-growth-mindset-is-crucial-for-business-leadership

Why leaders need a triple focus. (n.d.). Greater Good. https://greatergood.berkeley.edu/article/item/why_leaders_need_a_triple_focus

Yarwood, M. (n.d.). *Prefrontal cortex.* Pressbooks. https://psu.pb.unizin.org/psych425/chapter/prefrontal-cortex/

Yates, K. (Feb. 21, 2023). Using neuroplasticity for leadership. *Trevor Roberts.* https://blog.trevor-roberts.com.au/using-neuroplasticity-for-leadership